CW00971882

Table of Contents

Meet the Subject Matter Experts

Andrew Tjernlund

Amazon Consultant and Multi-Million Dollar Merchant

Andrew began his first importing business in 2005 at 19. Graduating as a double major with High Distinction from the Carlson School at 20, Andrew now owns and operates four businesses related to manufacturing, importing, private labeling, wholesale distribution, retail sales and third party marketplaces. His lifetime sales on eBay and Amazon are each in the 8 figures. His latest startup is www. AMZHelp.com which offers unlimited Amazon consulting from a team of experts for a monthly fee. Now 31, he lives in Hidden Hills Preserve with his wife and two young children.

Amanda Horner

Owner of CNH Pillow

Amanda Horner is the owner of CNH Pillow, Inc, a second-generation small family business. She is a firm believer that with the right information and tools, you can learn to do anything. Her other endeavors have included founding a non-profit children's home in India in 2006, becoming a certified henna artist in 2007, novel writing in 2011, and goat farming in 2015. She currently juggles home businesses, home making, and home schooling, and lives with her husband Craig and son Ed in central Texas.

Bryan Bowman

Founder, AMZ Profit Pros

Bryan Bowman is a private label seller with more than 10 years of entrepreneurship and ecommerce experience. He is a full-time traffic and conversion consultant for companies listing their products on Amazon and is passionate about helping sellers develop a successful online marketing strategy to take their businesses to the next level. When he's not working you'll usually find him on the mats training for a Brazilian Jiu Jitsu tournament.

James Thomson

Partner, Buy Box Experts

James Thomson is a partner at Buy Box Experts, a managed services agency supporting brands selling online. Earlier, he served as the business head of Amazon Services, the division of Amazon responsible for recruiting tens of thousands of sellers annually to the Amazon marketplace. He also served as the first Fulfillment by Amazon (FBA) account manager. Prior to Amazon, James was a management consultant and banker.

In 2015, James co-founded the PROSPER Show (prospershow.com), a continuing education conference for large Amazon sellers, and in 2017 published the book "The Amazon Marketplace Dilemma", designed for brand executives seeking to control their brands on the Amazon marketplace.

Eyal Lanxner

CTO, Feedvisor

Eyal Lanxner is CTO and Co-founder of Feedvisor. Prior to Feedvisor, Eyal managed the research and analytics groups at VeriSign and was CTO at Zoomix Data Mastering (acquired by Microsoft). Eyal holds a B.Sc. and M.Sc. in computer science from Bar-Ilan University, Israel.

Kevin Rizer

Founder, Private Label Podcast

Kevin Rizer is the host of Private Label Movement, rated the 'Best Amazon Podcast' by Amazon sellers in the 2017 Seller Awards. Kevin started his first brand selling physical products in 2014, and today has multiple six and seven figure brands. Private Label Movement reaches tens of thousands of sellers each month through the podcast, social media and events, and has become the authoritative source for information and inspiration on starting and building a brand.

Kai Klement

Co-founder and Managing Director of KAVAJ, Multi-Million Dollar Merchant

Kai Klement is the co-founder and managing director of KAVAJ GmbH and the KAVAJ Academy as well as the author of "The KAVAJ Case." KAVAJ is a manufacturer of high-quality genuine leather products for smartphones, tablets or wallets. Founded in October 2011, KAVAJ sells its products solely as a marketplace seller via Amazon (Europe, USA, Japan). KAVAJ has sold more than 500,000 KAVAJ products, making more than $19MM in revenue. Before founding KAVAJ, Kai Klement worked for 2.5 years as a Account Executive for Amazon.de in Munich, helping big Amazon sellers go international and sell more on Amazon.

Lauren Shepherd

Senior Marketing Manager,
Teikametrics

Kevin Rizer is the host of Private Label Movement, rated the 'Best Amazon Podcast' by Amazon sellers in the 2017 Seller Awards. Kevin started his first brand selling physical products in 2014, and today has multiple six and seven figure brands. Private Label Movement reaches tens of thousands of sellers each month through the podcast, social media and events, and has become the authoritative source for information and inspiration on starting and building a brand.

Tracey Wallace

Editor-in-Chief, BigCommerce

Tracey Wallace is the Editor in Chief at BigCommerce, where she runs BigCommerce's blog and case study program. She regularly talks and strategizes with brands making more than $5,000,000 in annual online revenue about what works and what doesn't.

Her insights and advice has been featured on MSNBC, Mashable, Entrepreneur, ELLE, Forbes, Refinery29 and Time Out New York.

Before BigCommerce, she helped grow two ecommerce brands to $1,000,000 in annual revenue through combined content and commerce strategies.

Yaffa Klugerman

Content Manager, Feedvisor

Yaffa Klugerman manages marketing content for Feedvisor, the Algo-Commerce company, which uses big data and machine learning algorithms to help online retailers make business-critical decisions. Prior to this role, she worked in public relations and marketing at the University of Michigan.

Forward

Bryan Eisenberg, New York Times Best Selling Author

In 2001, I was responsible for making sure our first self published book sold on Amazon. We didn't have much of a brand. We needed to be sure Persuasive Online Copywriting showed up when a customer searched for "online copywriting" books. Back then Amazon's algorithm was basic and simple.

They ranked you based primarily on the title of the product. Amazon's business and their algorithm have evolved. Today, Amazon wants to show their customers products and vendors who can for the most part "be like Amazon."

Factors such as customer service, product quality, speed to ship and handle returns are all part of the algorithm. These are a few of the examples of what makes a company be like Amazon. Specifically, in my latest book **Be Like Amazon: Even a Lemonade Stand Can Do It**, we highlight four pillars of success:

- Customer Centricity - focus on the customer experience
- Culture of Innovation - find new ways to add value to the customer
- Corporate Agility - speed of execution
- Continuous Improvement - be better today than you were yesterday.

These pillars are what drive Jeff Bezos' success in his B2B web services, his Washington Post acquisition and of course his retail business. In fact, it drives a lot of today's brands success. We want it to drive yours.

In **BigCommerce's Definitive Guide to Selling on Amazon**, you will pick up tips on techniques, tools and tactics that will boost you to the buy box. This guide is essential for anyone no how much experience they have selling on Amazon or anywhere online for that matter.

However, if you want to sustain that growth, Amazon will want to see how you are more like Amazon every day. They are defining the gold standard for today's customer experience.

In 2001, Jeff Bezos laid out his plan to conquer the retail world:

> *"We take those funds that might otherwise be used to shout about our service, and put those funds instead into improving the service. That's the philosophy we've taken from the beginning. — If you do build a great experience, customers tell each other about that. Word of mouth is very powerful."*

Building great customer experiences and generating great word of mouth, doesn't have to cost a lot of money. It does require an intense focus on details and an obsession with delighting customers.

So think of the four pillars as your new business operating system and **BigCommerce's Definitive Guide to Selling on Amazon** as your new operations manual for selling online.

To your continued success,
Bryan

Preface from BigCommerce

Tracey Wallace, Editor-in-Chief, BigCommerce

As a former journalist, the plethora of click-bait headlines across the web is nauseating. I've had to draw the line plenty of times in my writing career, refusing to call something "definitive," comprehensive" or "all-inclusive" if it wasn't that.

This piece of content required no such moral delineation.

This book's headline, Definitive Guide, is the only possible way to describe what you will find in the subsequent chapters. It is by far the most complete and actionable information out there discussing how exactly to sell on Amazon.

Here are some things you'll find throughout the book:

- How expanding to Amazon helped a Water Polo company successfully sell swimwear to Alaska
- Seven skills you must have to win on Amazon, as told to you by the former business head of Selling on Amazon
- How you could lose on Amazon by winning -- and other tips and tricks to avoid a double-sided sword
- Real examples of how to successfully sell on Amazon, when to use which strategies and growth hacking tips that edge on the side of controversial
- Pitfalls that trip up even the best Amazon sellers out there -- and how to avoid each and every one of them
- How to win the Buy Box, as told by Feedvisor, the unencumbered champion of Buy Box wins, where 82% of Amazon's sales happen
- Why mobile matters most -- 70% of Amazon customers made purchases on Amazon's mobile site -- and how to optimize for it

- Pricing and repricing strategies for both resellers and private label sellers alike -- plus tips to make you more, faster
- How to get a 320% increase in sales in less than 10 minutes (hint: Amazon has SEO, too)
- What The Mountain has to do with Amazon customer review legend -- and how you can jump start your own with a simple email
- A step-by-step guide to determining, once and for all, your actual Amazon revenue -- calculations and exactly what to measure are all included
- Growth hacking tips and tricks that could earn you $5,000 for every hour you spend focused on Amazon

This is actually the second publishing for this book -- and updated version for 2018. The original book was eight months in the making -- with the first email sent out to a subject matter expert on January 21, 2016, and that first book launching in August, 2016.

That timing is critical.

BigCommerce had just recently published the first ever Amazon Sellers' Solution Provider Directory -- highlighting more than 200 solution providers across a wide range of Amazon needs and complexities. It was our most downloaded piece of content at that time. James Thomson, former head of Selling on Amazon and an an author you'll see plenty of times throughout this book, was the mastermind behind that project. His name and proposal landed on my desk in the hibernation days between Christmas and New Years, when most Americans and almost all retailers are in the throes of a rest period following the holiday rush.

"I know it's the holidays, but please just hop on a call with him," a colleague pleaded. "You'll like what he has to say."

That 30-page book published two weeks later, forcing itself to the top of priority cycles that typically take much longer -- especially with multiple team members out on vacation. It was all hands on deck -- and I had called them there, asking many to spend a few extra hours to help me make this book come to life. I was putting my neck on the line -- calling in favors before the first day of the new year even began.

It was that good.

Soon, I was sending James emails asking him to review a table of contents for a longer-form, more comprehensive piece on how to sell on Amazon. It's safe to say that my call with James that late December day was a light bulb moment for me.

"This stuff is complex," I told him, "but the revenue opportunity for our customers is too ridiculous to ignore. Our merchants need the absolute best, most pertinent information to make this work. I won't waste their time."

He agreed, and the vetting process began. That first email went out. This 35,000+ word book had its first heartbeat of life. The 2016 version had 15 chapters, featuring the insights of more than 30 Amazon subject matter experts. This year's version for 2018 has XY chapters, featuring the insights of more than XY Amazon subject matter experts.

A few include:

- Andrew Tjernlund, Multi-Million Dollar Merchant and Amazon Consultant
- Andy Geldman, Editor-in-Chief, Web Retailer
- Bryan Bowman, Founder, AMZ Profit Pros
- Eyal Lanxner, CTO, Feedvisor
- James Thomson, Partner at the Buy Box Experts, Founder of The PROSPER Show, Former Head of Selling on Amazon
- Kai Klement, Co-founder and Multi-Million Dollar Merchant, KAVAJ
- Kevin Rizer, Founder, Private Label Podcast
- Lauren, Shepherd, Senior Marketing Manager, Teikametrics
- Ohad Hagai, VP Marketing, Feedvisor

We left no stone unturned, nor did we include any information we believed to be superfluous. You will find everything you need to start selling and winning on Amazon in this book. I can also assure you it will be a vital resource you continue to reference as you grow Amazon as a revenue channel. Even for those sellers already highly profitable on Amazon, there are nuggets of insight to even further increase sales and operationalize your Amazon business.

What are you waiting for? Dive in. Take action. Grow your business. And let us know if you have any questions.

This book will be a living and breathing document. We will be updating this Definitive guide, adding or removing information to make sure you have everything you need to sell more on Amazon today and in the future.

This is for your 2018 journey. We'll see next year as we republish our 2019 one. To now, to future-proofing, to the year ahead.

01 The Case for Multi-Channel Selling: Expansion and Optimization

Tracey Wallace, Editor-in-Chief, BigCommerce

The world is full of famous rivalries. Coke vs. Pepsi. Windows vs. Mac. Godzilla vs. Mothra.

And, used to be, marketplaces vs. webstores.

It's a story nearly as infamous as David and Goliath –– independent websites trying to keep their head above water when it comes to the power and visibility of marketplaces like Amazon. It's romantic to think of independent sellers as the underdogs, an agile kid going up against a powerful giant –– little hope in his court. That is if that were the actual story of David and Goliath.

It isn't.

See, David was never an underdog. Goliath was always set to lose. It's human inaccuracy that has long gotten the story mixed up.

"So here [David] is, this shepherd, experienced in the use of a devastating weapon, up against this lumbering giant weighed down by a hundred pounds of armor and these incredibly heavy weapons that are useful only in short-range combat," tells Malcolm Gladwell. "Goliath is a sitting duck. He doesn't have a chance."

Innovation is what made David successful. It's our misunderstanding of his choice of weaponry that confounds us and makes us think he was ever an underdog. No, he instead was using modern technology and agility to his favor -- easily ousting the giant before the giant could comprehend the situation at hand. This metaphor isn't to say Amazon and your independent webstore are David or Goliath. No, your business gets to choose whether it will be David or Goliath.

- Will you diversify?
- Will you use all the modern tools at your disposal to come out ahead?
- Or, will you choose to stand there, armored in and weighed down.
- Will you choose to be a sitting duck -- or will you decide to pull out your slingshot?

What if you could have a recognizable brand, selling through your own store and at the same time use Amazon to drive additional sales?

That would be the best of both worlds, wouldn't it?

That would make you David -- and that's what this guide is all about. This book will show you that it's not only possible to sell on both marketplaces and your own webstore, but that it helps build a stronger, larger and more profitable business.

It's a Multi-Channel World After All

If you go to ecommerce meetups or conferences, you can pick up on single-channel thinking in the way people speak.

They'll often say "I'm an Amazon seller" or "I have my own online store." Now and again someone will say, "I'm a multi-channel seller," but most of the time they equate their business with the channel they sell through. You don't hear that from consumers. From their point of view, the world is intrinsically multi-channel.

They don't say, "I'm an Amazon buyer," or "I only buy from independent webstores." (Well, only very rarely!) They just love the convenience, choice, price, and overall experience of online shopping – wherever that may take them. Of course, everyone has their preferences, but few will insist on only ever buying through one channel. As of February 2017, Amazon accounted for 43% of U.S. online retail sales. And that's growing. Fortune predict Amazon sales will account for more than 50% of all US ecommerce sales by 2021.

That's a huge chunk of the market for just one companies. But it doesn't tell the whole story. Sure, Amazon is a retailer in its own right, but 51% of its unit sales are from third-party merchants – up from 48% this time last year alone. So yes, Amazon occupies a vast space in ecommerce, but it's a space that's accessible to everyone. Online marketplaces are wonderfully convenient for consumers, but only because of the large number of third-party sellers already doing business there.

There's also plenty of pie left for independent ecommerce.

Within the 57% of the market not belonging to Amazon, there is of course other large companies (Jet, Walmart, Alibaba), but there's also a buzzing independent ecommerce market. BigCommerce's own research estimates that ecommerce SMBs will exceed $100 billion in total annual sales. Both online marketplaces and independent ecommerce stores are huge, but their success and your success are not mutually exclusive. What would it do for your business if you could succeed at both?

Marketplaces are from Mars; Webstores are from Venus

Online marketplaces and independent webstores operate very differently. It's easy to understand why businesses which succeed in one can be dismissive of the other.
Here's a breakdown of some of the biggest differences.

#1: MARKETPLACE KNOWLEDGE

Marketplace sellers become very skilled in navigating all the rules, processes and policies of the platforms they use.
- **When you sell through marketplaces,** they make the rules, and you have to follow them.
- **Independent sellers,** however, are used to playing the game their own way. The labyrinthine marketplace requirements can be frustrating for them.

#2: COMPETITION AND PRICE

Marketplaces are highly competitive places by design. Sellers have to compete very hard on price but find reward with higher sales volumes.

Therefore, financial proficiency is crucial, and successful sellers become very skilled at managing their margins and squeezing one or two extra percentage points by cutting costs or automating processes. Independent sellers can be overwhelmed by the intensity of competition, and the loss of control over pricing.

#3: SALES VOLUME

Marketplaces are tightly controlled and extremely competitive, but they have one thing in spades: **ready and willing buyers.**

Their endless rules are there to provide a consistent, high-quality experience for consumers. The competitive environment has sellers fighting to deliver the best prices and service. And all those varied sellers give rise to a very broad product selection. **It's a recipe that buyers love:** Play the marketplaces game well and you'll get big sales with very little external marketing effort.

#4: FEES

It is not a free ride. Marketplaces charge substantial fees for all that exposure. Their fee structures can be complicated, but 12% to 15% of the sale price is fairly typical.

You pay that day in and day out, on each and every sale.

That being said, selling on your own webstore is not free either. You have to pay to process every sale there, as well. As you know, it varies based on your payment gateway, the method of payment from your customer, and their location, among other factors.

#5: CONTROL

Finally, this brings us to the core benefit of having your own webstore: control. With your own independent storefront you can:

- Give your store a unique brand personality.
- Present your products in whichever way works best.
- Let your imagination run wild with marketing tactics.
- Show expert knowledge of your product niche.
- Distance yourself from competitors' pricing.

And your webstore customers belong to you. You have their order history and data on how they use your site, what items are in their shopping cart, and what pages they are viewing. You can now market to them directly, which is powerful when done properly.

- Marketplaces have amazing potential to generate sales at a predictable, fixed cost.
- Webstores have equally amazing potential to build a brand and make repeat sales – at a less predictable, but decreasing cost.

Different Strokes for Different Folks

Online marketplaces and independent webstores can be complementary sales channels, but you might need to take a different approach to each one. Your webstore requires in-depth communication with your customer and ever-changing marketing that speaks to their wants and desires. On a marketplace, customers are just as important -- you'll need reviews and sales to increase your Amazon page ranking, for instance -- but you as the seller are one step removed.

That aside, here's multi-channel selling in a nutshell:

1. Put all your inventory data into a single system.
2. Publish that data to as many sales channels as possible.
3. Sit back and wait for the orders to come in.

That's it. Technology is an enabler that sets up and maintains the correct data on different sales channels, and brings all the orders back to one place for processing. For businesses who sell through their own webstore, putting all their data onto a shared platform like Amazon can be a frightening proposition.

That fear is not unwarranted.

Not only will your inventory be exposed to thousands of competitors, but Amazon themselves will see exactly how well all your products sell. They're not shy of competing with their own third-party sellers, and when Amazon competes, Amazon usually wins. The solution is straightforward: you don't have to sell everything everywhere.

DO YOU HAVE POPULAR PRODUCTS THAT YOU CAN OFFER AT A MARKET-LEADING PRICE?

Put those on Amazon, and use them to generate a healthy cash flow. Consumers will find them there anyway, so it might as well be you who gets the sale.

THEN CONSIDER IF YOU HAVE ANY HARD-TO-FIND PRODUCTS THAT CUSTOMERS WILL SEEK OUT.

Keep those on your own site, and use them to bring in new buyers – well away from the glare of Amazon's floodlights. These are products that help make your store unique, so there's no need to give Amazon a cut. In the next chapter, we'll take a look at businesses already successfully selling on Amazon and their own store.

02 Selling Swimwear to Alaskans: The True Story of How 3 Brands Expanded on Amazon

Tracey Wallace, Editor-in-Chief, BigCommerce

It was a typical work day for Alex Young in 2012.

He was at the Kap7 headquarters, his employer's office. It was lunch time, a Wednesday maybe. He had a friend's event that weekend and needed something ... shoes, a pair of pants. It doesn't really matter, because, as usual, he was shopping on Amazon. A tried, tested and trusted 2-day delivery was in his grasp. It didn't matter what he bought, or how late he bought it; he knew he would be able to get the item in his hands for when he needed it.

In fact, Alex and the rest of his co-workers, including the former Olympian founders of the company, Wolf Wigo and Brad Schumacher, all regularly shopped on Amazon. And they did this while running their own, independent online store.

On one of those quick Amazon shopping days, Alex did a query for the product his company sold:

"Water Polo Ball"

It's hard to say what Alex saw years ago, but today, you do a similar search and two brands clearly dominate on Amazon:

1. Misaka
2. Alex's own Kap7.

And Kap7 is the only one that is NCAA and NFHS official. Kap7 also sells water polo swimwear, so I did a quick search for that, too. This small, 7-person company headquartered in L.A. comes up third on Amazon, right behind Nike.

That's one heck of a search engine optimization success story.

> *"We were personally shopping on Amazon all the time, and there wasn't anyone that was selling our type of products there," says Alex.*

> *"We needed to take advantage of that. None of our direct competitors have moved onto Amazon yet, so we are ahead of the game in the water polo market. Once you have it dialed-in [to Amazon], it runs itself."*

Alex thinks about Amazon as simply another sales channel for his business. Of course, Amazon does play by different rules than a typical webstore.

For instance, Kap7 can often make 50% margin off of its products. On Amazon, that may go down to 25%. But a 50% decrease in margins for a highly trafficked and high sales channel doesn't cause a bit of concern for Alex and his team. They have full control over their marketplace selling, understand the industry and when it will spike, and know that different customers shop in vastly different ways.

For Kap7, control, sales and buyer personas make the expansion to Amazon a success — and a no-brainer.

> *"There are people who only shop on Amazon, and there are people who want to shop on direct ecommerce sites. Both sets of people are growing," says Alex.*

> *"Water polo is growing extremely fast in the U.S., and we can get spikes in orders. If we get low on inventory for a product we have to order in bulk, like balls, we will turn off our marketplaces and keep selling on our website."*

This level of control and ability to turn on and off selling options on Amazon as needed gives the Kap7 team, and Alex in particular, the freedom to use the webstore in unique ways. For Alex, Amazon revenue is a known. It will come in. People are shopping there. On a webstore, it's a different story.

Amazon already has an audience. Independent websites must build an audience -- and that's tough work. But with Amazon as a steady source of income, Alex has figured out how to use additional tools -- like Google AdWords and Google Shopping -- to target consumers elsewhere on the web and bring them back to a dedicated website targeting their specific needs.

After all, you can customize a website to serve a buyer's persona. With Amazon, you're going for keywords and mass relevance.

> *"We do a lot of marketing to the end-user, who is the age-group athlete, and then the purchaser who is the parents. We try to loop things around with product reviews and videos, and water polo drills and tips," says Alex.*

> *"We use BigCommerce to power our ecommerce website, which also gives us more opportunity to focus on really specific groups. For example, we focused on selling Alaska-printed suits to people in Alaska using Google AdWords, and they sold really well for about six months."*

That's right, the combined power of Amazon and independent webstore earned a water polo company in L.A. a buying audience in Alaska. That's how to optimize sales channels.

Uncovering 100% Growth on Amazon through Search

We're in L.A. again. This time, in the home of Emily Ironi, the sole founder and employee of The Dairy Fairy -- a quickly growing nursing bra company serving the likes of Zoe Saldana and Chrissy Teigen. But this is no celebrity-only brand. Little over four years ago, Emily Ironi was a new, working and single mom. And like any parent, she wanted to give her kid the best shot at life.

To her, breastfeeding was a part of that legacy. The selection of nursing bras she found, however, were not. To Emily, they looked like medieval torture devices.

- They weren't attractive.
- They weren't comfortable.
- And even though they did the job, allowing a woman to breastfeed with a bra on, they left much to be desired.

For one, postpartum is real -- and no new mom wants to be made to feel unattractive simply by trying to feed her baby. For two, the pointy and uncomfortable nature made nursing bras near impossible to actually wear as a bra. Instead, you'd need to wear another bra, and then change into the nursing bras before nursing to achieve maximum comfort and functionality from what was on the market. No one has time for any of that.

So, Emily made her own bra -- patent pending.

Today, new moms and older ones alike wear that bra, many of them choosing to continue wearing the bra beyond breastfeeding thanks to its comfort, support and ... well ... let's just say it's pretty. In 2013, she launched her online store -- and immediately, sales began rolling in. She'd found a niche market. Customers were finding her by Google and bloggers. Then, in October of 2015, she looked to Amazon and launched a test run.

Sales doubled.

> *"Amazon's been incredible for my business. I started selling on Amazon in October of 2015, and it's doubled my sales," says Emily. "What that tells me is that there's a whole slew of people who didn't know I existed, and they'd just go in and type 'hands-free pumping bra.' It's working way better than a Google search for me."*

Amazon search outperforming Google's isn't surprising. Research has shown that 44% of all product searches start on Amazon. If you rely solely on Google search to bring in customers, your first competitor to sell on Amazon will mop up all the buyers that search there first -- much like Kap7 did.

Think about it.

Amazon is a search engine for products that likely has your credit card on file, allowing you to checkout in a single click. It's arguably the easiest shopping destination in the world. If you have an audience that is busy (and all of us are), Amazon is the quickest, most convenient shopping solution for them.

That doesn't mean, though, that your own website isn't relevant.

> *"Amazon as a business is becoming more of a competitor to some of the brands, and bringing out their own products," says Emily. "I find that it's still critical to have your own retail presence. I have a lot of peers, especially in the baby products industry, their businesses were 100% on Amazon, and now they're starting to catch up and trying to migrate more of their business to their own websites."*

> *"Ultimately, you have a lot more control over everything and also your interaction with customers. It's about finding that perfect balance."*

Customer's Choice: Using Data to Sell the Products They Want Where they Want Them

Relative to Austin Bazaar, The Dairy Fairy and Kap7 are newbies to Amazon. Seetha Singh, the owner of the instrument retailer, launched her webstore almost simultaneously with her Amazon presence back in 2007 -- nearly a decade ago. Her goal then and now is still them same: be wherever the customer is. Cost-effectiveness is high on her list as well.

> *"We wanted to be present wherever customers for our products like to shop," says Seetha. "Selling direct and via third party channels has helped us broaden our reach. Selling on Amazon affords us the benefit of reaching millions of Amazon customers without spending the advertising dollars up-front."*

And as you might expect from such a seasoned Amazon seller, Seetha has drafted a comprehensive multi-channel strategy for Austin Bazaar. The company's Amazon success is no fluke. It took years of sales data and multiple iterations in the analyzing to determine which products sell best on the channel, and how to optimize each selling point for the highest conversion.

> *"We do not offer the same products on all channels," says Seetha. "We offer our best selections on our webstore, but also have products that are unique to each channel. The selection offered on each channel depends on the strengths of that channel and the kind of consumers that they attract." "By offering specialized inventory on our webstore, we are better able to mitigate the effects of cannibalization that can occur when multi-channel selling."*

For Seetha, marketplaces like Amazon are just the right places to be. Too many consumers are already shopping there for any retailer to ignore it. Getting in front of your customers in the way they want to shop is the most important part of selling success.

Your website can offer the who, what, when, where and why -- but your customers get the final say in how.

Too Much of a Good Thing

Know this: Amazon is not a set-it-and-forget-it channel. You can go too big. It's possible you'll need to pull back. But then again, is that the worst problem to have?

> *"Make sure you are focused on the channels you already have in place, so they are running themselves. Then step over to the next channel and build that," says Alex.*

> *"The biggest mistake we made is we tried to go full-bore on all of them – Etsy, Jet, eBay. We've*

actually pulled it all back because we want to focus on each one, make sure it's perfect and understand why products are selling well, or not."

"Once they're running well it's just a management and maintenance scenario, which is not that big of a deal."

First, do the competitor research; then launch in the channel; finally use product data to optimize. That's how these three companies are seeing 100%+ growth in revenue coming from their Amazon channel, plus extra time and money to spend on acquiring new audiences for their independent webstore. It's isn't a no-sum game. In fact, it's a winner takes all –– and the winner is the retailer.

The winner is you.

03 Is Your Business a Good Fit for Amazon?

James Thomson, PROSPER Show Founder

Amazon has made its marketplace welcoming for newcomers.

New sellers will find a platform where it takes only minutes to sign up, and a few more minutes beyond that to get product listings live on the site. With Amazon's intent to attract as much selection as possible to the marketplace, it makes sense that Amazon wants to make it functionally easy for anyone to start listing products on its site.

Yet, the decision to sell on Amazon should not be based just on ease of signup.

Sellers also a need a clear understanding of what it takes to have a realistic chance of being successful on Amazon. While Amazon still attracts general merchandise resellers that offer the same products as many other companies, the long-term success of those sorts of companies is very much in question. In a battle of margins and trying to differentiate in a meaningful way, sellers may end up working harder and harder each year to generate the same top line sales, and possibly not the same bottom line revenue.

Before we dive in to discuss which types of businesses are most likely to be successful on Amazon, let's first review a few fundamentals about the Amazon marketplace to help you determine product fit.

What Sellers Need to Know About Amazon

ALMOST ANYONE CAN LIST PRODUCTS FOR SALE ON AMAZON

Unless a brand has tight distribution controls over its product, it's not unusual to find dozens – if not hundreds – of resellers offering the same products on Amazon.

This crowding creates price competition, as well as incentives to ignore MAP/MSRP pricing policies or to divert products at low margins, just to get some margin out of holding a particular brand.

AMAZON SETS THE RULES OF ITS OWN MARKETPLACE

Amazon has given itself the advantage of collecting massive amounts of customer search and customer purchase data, with which it shares only the minimum amounts with sellers.

This compendium of information gives Amazon's first-party business – Amazon Retail, i.e. private label – a huge advantage of picking winners over and over when targeting products that it should sell itself on the marketplace.

Furthermore, Amazon Retail will almost always win the Buy Box, which is the mechanism through which sellers competing on the same product will get ranked to determine who gets the sale when the customer clicks the "Add to Cart" button.

So if a seller is competing head-to-head with Amazon on a product, it's not likely the seller will get many sales, given that Amazon Retail has the Buy Box advantage. Amazon Retail also has sophisticated re-pricing software which allows it to lower prices to match prices already lowered by competing sellers. And, with Amazon Retail content not making any money (or even losing money) on a sale, it is not likely that a competing seller will either get the sale from Amazon Retail or make any margin from the sale.

Bottom Line: Competing directly on the same listings that Amazon Retail offers is not likely to be an effective business model long-term.

AMAZON WANTS ITS SELLERS TO USE "FULFILLMENT BY AMAZON" (FBA)

FBA is Amazon's fulfillment program that's offered too all third-party sellers. Sellers put their products into Amazon's network of fulfillment centers, and when a customer places an order, Amazon does the individual order fulfillment, rather than the seller.

Such products in FBA are eligible for Amazon Prime / Amazon Super Saver Shipping, two programs that have consistently been found to improve most sellers' customer conversion rates. While a seller may have world-class fulfillment capabilities of its own, this FBA advantage is granted as part of Amazon's efforts to ensure the highest quality, consistent shopping experience for Amazon customers.

WHEN A SELLER ON AMAZON GETS ORDERS, IT DOES NOT OWN THE CUSTOMER RELATIONSHIP.

Each sale is viewed as a one-time transaction, and **sellers aren't allowed to market or re-market to these customers after the sale.**

So while sellers may have sophisticated CRM capabilities for their non-Amazon channels, almost all of that skill and technology is irrelevant for customers generated through the Amazon marketplace.

AMAZON MAKES CLEAR THAT IT IS EXCLUSIVELY THE RESPONSIBILITY OF THE BRAND TO SECURE ITS DISTRIBUTION

Namely, Amazon will rarely get involved in helping brands to remove unauthorized resellers, thereby implicitly encouraging anyone to sell any product on Amazon, as long as it is a legitimate product where no harm is inflicted on the Amazon customer.

EVERY SELLER ON AMAZON IS REQUIRED TO ANSWER CUSTOMER INQUIRIES WITHIN 24 HOURS

This requirement applies to any day of the year. And Amazon holds every seller to the highest industry standards regarding shipping times, confirmation emails, order cancellation rates and a slew of other criteria. For many businesses new to Amazon, these standards may well be beyond what they can handle, and hence the Amazon marketplace may be too much for them to handle. So with these conditions in place, let's discuss how different sorts of businesses are likely to do on the Amazon marketplace.

How Different Business Models Work on Amazon

THE RESELLER: NO EXCLUSIVE SOURCING RELATIONSHIPS

Unless a reseller with no exclusive sourcing relationships has a significant pricing advantage, it's not likely that this type of seller will be able to get any more than its fair share of sales from Amazon. In other words, if this type of seller is competing against nine other resellers, this individual seller isn't likely to get more than 10% of the sales -- unless it's willing to undercut everyone else on price.

A race to the bottom on price eventually lowers margins to an unsustainable level, making it pointless to be selling on Amazon. For the general retail business considering offering some of its products on Amazon, this channel is likely to be only a secondary channel if all of your catalog is readily available to any number of other retailers.

As an Amazon reseller, it's critical for you to have paperwork that shows a clear provenance of where you sourced product.

While some gray market sellers may do well on Amazon, once Amazon's Seller Performance team challenges them – asking them to provide paperwork showing where the product came from – the seller may not be able to address a claim of selling counterfeit or inauthentic product. And, even for sellers with solid paperwork from manufacturers or authorized distributors, Amazon may still give the seller a hard time if too many customer complaints come in about the legitimacy of the product.

THE RESELLER: EXCLUSIVE SOURCING RELATIONSHIPS

If the seller has negotiated exclusive sourcing relationships from specific brands with decent control of their distribution, preventing any number of unauthorized or gray-market sellers from also selling on Amazon, then this seller is likely to do well as it doesn't have to compete with other sellers for the "buy box."

While the principle of an exclusive sourcing relationship makes a lot of sense for sellers, few brands understand the dynamics of the Amazon marketplace well enough to be willing to limit who can sell on Amazon.

This lack of understanding can potentially result in less product sold to retailers in the short-term.

Such sellers typically have to agree to represent the brands well on Amazon, by way of improving listing content, ensuring MAP/MSRP prices are in place, and keeping inventory levels adequately stocked for the Amazon customer demand. With the advent of the FBA program, **it is becoming easier for brands to go direct-to-consumer with their own seller accounts on Amazon, cutting out resellers altogether.**

For brands that are willing to handle some day-to-day operational responsibilities (or outsource these responsibilities to agencies), they can make retail margins selling direct-to-consumers on Amazon, rather than securing only wholesale margins selling to retailers/resellers that will, in turn, sell on Amazon.

THE SELLER OF OVERSIZED OR HAZMAT PRODUCTS

While Amazon does allow sellers to offer oversized and hazmat products to Amazon customers, the cost or FBA restrictions may be such that it doesn't make financial sense for such companies to sell on Amazon. If you are such a company, we encourage you to do extensive research on Amazon before signing up to be an Amazon seller.

THE PRIVATE LABEL SELLER

In the past five years, there has been a huge increase in the number of sellers on Amazon that are building their own brands (often through inexpensive overseas sourcing, e.g., AlibabaCombing Amazon product reviews and sales rank data of national brands, these sellers identify product or price gaps that they believe they can fill with their own, newly-developed private label brands.

Typically, these sellers can enjoy 3-6 months of decent sales before their products do well enough to be identified by other private label sellers to target for their own private label versions. f the private label seller becomes effective at evolving its catalog quickly and capitalizing in the short-term on its newly launched products, such a seller can do reasonably well on Amazon.

THE NATIONAL BRAND

If a brand has created decent customer awareness, chances are some share of 300 million Amazon customers have already been looking for the brand on Amazon. Unable to find it, they move on to a competitor brand.

For such a national brand, it makes a lot of sense to be evaluating Amazon as an incremental sales channel. If the brand launches a seller account, using high-quality content in its listings coupled with some advertising budget to drive awareness of its presence on Amazon, such a brand can build its Amazon business into a decent channel.

Yes, there may be **some cannibalization from its other channels, but we have found that the vast majority of sales on Amazon are incremental,** given just how many Amazon customers there are, and how few of them are likely to have shopped on the brand's own website.

For brands that have a regional awareness, it will take more time to build up a business on Amazon, but the underlying distribution control is most critical to the brand being able to sell its product on Amazon, without plenty of other resellers competing for the same sale.

If a brand is successful with the Amazon channel, then the benefits of incremental sales at retail margins should produce solid financial results for the brand.

Final Word

Any brand of any size on Amazon must recognize that it will earn certain rights on Amazon if the brand has a registered trademark, GS1-sourced UPC codes, and branding on both the packaging and physical product.

For many brands new to Amazon, they are surprised to see that Amazon will not always respect the brand's efforts to legitimize itself as a brand unless it has secured these aforementioned product and legal characteristics.

Also, the day-to-day operations of running an Amazon seller business must be properly addressed, given how high the performance standards are to which Amazon holds its sellers.

In subsequent chapters, we'll cover how to meet these requirements and put operational processes in place.

04 How Not to Sell on Amazon, According to the Former Head of Selling on Amazon

James Thomson, PROSPER Show Founder

The Amazon marketplace is designed to make it easy for practically anyone to list products on the site, including the brands themselves. Add the features of the FBA program, and now companies that haven't historically fulfilled direct-to-consumer orders can easily handle that operational complexity.

Layer in how Amazon's Buy Box algorithm prefers lower-priced offers to higher-priced ones and competition across different sellers can quickly become a race to the bottom for margins. With far too many sellers not properly incorporating all of their costs into their pricing decisions, I regularly see sellers overestimating how far they can drop their prices and still be profitable. **Brands acting as direct-to-consumer resellers on Amazon are better able to cut retail prices and remain profitable, creating an advantage over resellers.**

So, it becomes harder for a reseller to bring meaningful value to customers if:

- There is no real limit to how many resellers could offer the same products
- Resellers are having to undercut one another on price to win the Buy Box
- They don't often understand their all-in cost structures
- The very brands that make product available to them are now able to compete side-by-side as resellers, often under disguised seller names

Only those resellers having an exclusive sourcing relationship with its brands, where the brands also agree not to become resellers themselves, have much luck with this route. Even so, as more brands realize the opportunity on Amazon, fewer brands are willing to make such a deal. In response to these many changes, we have seen two major shifts in the past 3-4 years occur among the base of resellers on Amazon:

1. Resellers are aggressively courting brands to become their exclusive resellers on Amazon
2. Resellers are developing private label brands of their own so that they can become exclusive resellers of their own brands.

With so many new private label brands surfacing, there is no longer just competition across national brands or between national brands and private label brands, but now also between private label brands operating in the same product spaces.

So if you're about to get started on Amazon as a third-party seller, it's critical to understand what sourcing/distribution advantages you will have, as those gains are likely to be short-lived. t's critical for third-party sellers to continuously evaluate their product sourcing advantages and expect that the products making the seller profitable today will need to evolve into a different mix of products within six months.

How Amazon Wins on Amazon

There are more than 2,000,000 third-party sellers operating on the Amazon marketplace. And yet, Amazon has all the data, including but not limited to:

- Which products customers search for
- What they actually buy
- How much they buy at what prices
- Where they can't find the brands they were searching for

Although Amazon is a publicly held company, it's investors have **tolerated years of razor-thin margins,** which has partly played out by way of Amazon selling products at next to no profit or even at unprofitable levels.

Amazon would make more profit in the short-term by letting third-party sellers earn the sale. However, the company has taken the approach, in each category of products, of pursuing all of the strategic brands it believes need to be in the catalog to attract Amazon customers to shop first on Amazon over any other site –– online or offline. To do this, **Amazon has made a number of sourcing agreements with brands to acquire products at prices that don't enable Amazon to make any significant profit.**

This is because the objectives here are for Amazon to bring the right selection at prices consistent with or lower than market prices, available all of the time to Amazon customers. To make these objectives possible, **Amazon has chosen selectively to forgo short-term profits in pursuit of long-term customer loyalty.**

For the third-party seller competing head-to-head with Amazon Retail, these differences in objectives often create situations where Amazon lowers its prices to a point where, rightfully so, the third-party sellers competing against Amazon can't figure out how Amazon Retail is making any money.

The answer is that Amazon isn't making money, at least in the short-term, and it's entirely comfortable with that.

I have also seen third-party sellers frustrated that Amazon doesn't increase its prices in times of scarcity, such as popular toys being sold right before Christmas. In these situations, while Amazon may put limits on how much product any one customer can buy, it maintains prices at stable levels to help Amazon customers avoid apparent price gouging that can happen otherwise in such situations. Let's just say that Amazon's runway is a lot longer than any of the other sellers on Amazon.

Finally, for FBA sellers whose products end up competing directly with Amazon Retail, these sellers often get frustrated that they rarely win the "Buy Box," even though their products are also Amazon Prime eligible (by being FBA products) and sold at the same prices as Amazon or even slightly lower.

Yes, **as long as Amazon is in stock on an item, it will almost always win the Buy Box,** even if another seller appears to have a better price and equal Amazon Prime designation on its offer. At some point, another seller can lower its prices below a threshold that Amazon Retail has set for itself, but that point is usually well under water for all sellers. This information isn't to scare you away from Amazon. In fact, it's here to do exactly the opposite. Knowing how to operate your business within the Amazon ecosystem will better help you to win in this massive global channel. Competing directly with Amazon Retail isn't necessarily a winning strategy, but there are plenty of other strategies to double down on or modify your approach.

The rest of this guide will expand on each of those.

05

A Handy Amazon Seller Account Setup Checklist

James Thomson, PROSPER Show Founder

The moment you sign up for an Amazon seller account, the clock starts.

> **With your first monthly account charge coming through after 30 days, you are expected to meet all Amazon performance metrics from day one.**

Before you jump in headfirst and start selling on Amazon, there are several steps we encourage any prospective seller to take before formalizing the seller account registration process.

The Necessary Paperwork — an Amazon Checklist

To get through the full registration process for an Amazon seller account, you will need a bunch of information readily available, including:

- **Business Information**

  Your legal business name, address, and contact information

- **Email Address**

  An email address that can be used for this company account. This email account should be set up already, as you will start receiving important emails from Amazon almost immediately.

- **Credit Card**

  An internationally-chargeable credit card with a valid billing address. If the credit card number isn't valid, Amazon will cancel your registration.

- **Phone Number**

  A phone number where you can be reached during this registration process. Also, have your phone nearby during registration.

- **Tax ID**

  Your tax identity information, including your Social Security number or your company's Federal Tax ID number. To submit your tax identity information, the registration process will take a brief detour to a "1099-K Tax Document Interview."

- **State Tax ID**

  State tax ID information for states in which you have tax nexus. This physical presence is typically impacted by company offices, warehouses/3PLs, and call centers. If you plan to use Amazon's Fulfillment by Amazon (FBA) program, there may be further tax nexus implications. I encourage you to talk with a tax attorney or tax accountant who specializes in online seller tax nexus issues (e.g., catchingclouds.net, peisnerjohnson.com) or one of the tax remittance that can give you the most current Amazon tax nexus information (e.g., taxjar.com, avalara.com, taxify.co, vertexsmb.com).

- **Passport Information**

  Amazon requires all new seller account owners to provide their passport information to confirm their identity. This rule applies to sellers whether they are based inside or outside the US.

Questions to Work Through Before Registering Your Seller Account

Some of the logistics of being a successful seller should be worked out before you set up the seller account, as you likely won't have as much time to address these after you get started.

WHERE DO YOU PLAN TO SEND ORDER RETURNS?

Are you going to handle the returns yourself, or send them to a company that specializes in testing/grading returns and making the product available for sale again (e.g., tradeport.com, openedboxreturns.com)

WHO ON YOUR TEAM WILL HANDLE AMAZON CUSTOMER INQUIRIES?

The key is not just having all of the answers, but also respecting Amazon's requirements to respond to all customer inquiries within 24 hours, any day of the year. Hence, figuring out who is on point (with possible backup) is one critical operational issue that should be addressed before opening your Amazon seller account.

IF YOU PLAN TO USE AMAZON'S FULFILLMENT BY AMAZON PROGRAM, WILL YOU CO-MINGLE YOUR PRODUCTS?

I very much recommend using FBA, given its visibility potential to 50MM+ Amazon Prime customers. If you decide to go that route, you'll need to decide whether you plan to co-mingle your products with FBA inventory of other sellers of the same products.

Amazon gives FBA sellers this potentially lethal option of sending product into Amazon's Fulfillment Centers, where they might get co-mingled with other FBA sellers' product, leading to your products possibly getting mixed up with counterfeit or low-grade versions of what you purport to be selling. Unfortunately, if a co-mingled unit gets picked to fulfill an order on your account, you are left explaining to Amazon why a customer complained about getting a counterfeit item.

You need to work through this issue very early on because if you decide to use FBA but not use the co-mingled ("stickerless") option, you need to activate your account to become a "stickered" FBA account right at the beginning before you create your first FBA shipment into Amazon. While it is possible later on to become a stickered account, it quickly becomes very complicated if you have already sent some product into FBA as stickerless product.

DO YOU PLAN TO USE A DBA (DOING BUSINESS AS) NAME TO OPERATE YOUR AMAZON SELLER ACCOUNT?

While some companies have legitimate reasons to use a different customer-facing name, Amazon is also a place where many sellers purposefully conceal their identity.

Reasons for doing this include not wanting brands to know that they are selling online, or the brand is actually the reseller and doesn't want its other retail partners to know it's selling product online direct to consumer.

HAVE YOU CHECKED TO SEE IF THE PRODUCTS YOU PLAN TO LIST ARE IN CATEGORIES THAT AMAZON HAS GATED?

Amazon has restrictions on who can sell in certain categories, and while the ungating process is usually surmountable, it's important to recognize that if your desired categories are gated, you will have to apply very quickly to get ungated.

Check out Amazon's approval category page before you decide to register on Amazon, and you can learn more about the ungating process if it applies to your product categories.

Amazon has already started gating specific brands and SKUs.

During your first 30 days with a seller account, we encourage you to add all of your intended catalog to your Amazon seller account. You will quickly be able to establish whether you will have problems with specific brands and SKUs. You may need to change your catalog or close your account if Amazon is restricting the products you intended to sell.

Skills You Should Know Now – Or Understand How to Build Quickly

The Amazon marketplace has its own setup rules and regulations, but also its own combination of skills that every seller should master fairly quickly to succeed profitably and long-term.

These include:

STELLAR MARKETING CONTENT TO BUILD PRODUCT LISTINGS

If the products you are selling are already sold by others on Amazon, this is less important because you will most likely end up adding your offer to the product listing that's already in place (requiring you to provide only basic pricing, quantity available and SKU name information).

But, if your products are new to the Amazon catalog (easy to check by simply searching for your brand or UPC in the Amazon.com search bar), you will need to come up with content for such field as product titles, bullet points, product description, and generic keywords (for optimizing SEO on your listings).

You will also need product images for your listings – check out Amazon's adding images support page for reference, but we encourage sellers to have multiple images, including a lifestyle image, if possible, to show the product in use. This lifestyle image complements the main image that has strict requirements, including a white background, no branding and at least a 500x500 pixel count.

CLEAR UNDERSTANDING OF YOUR PRODUCT SOURCING AVENUES

If your products sell well on Amazon, do you know how to replenish quickly enough to avoid extensive stockout periods? If you specialize in close-outs and one-time buys, you may not be able to replenish the same SKUs easily, but should have strong channels for adding new inventory, as your Amazon cash position improves.

A DECISION ON IF YOU PLAN TO SELL THE SAME ITEMS OVER AND OVER

If yes, you will want to take advantage of Amazon's replenishment alert tools inside Seller Central, as well as other external forecasting tools, such as standalone tools from www.forecastly.com or those integrated into many of the multichannel inventory/order management tools.

A DEVELOPED PROCESS FOR IDENTIFYING AND ADDRESSING STALE INVENTORY

While everyone wants their products to sell, the reality is there will always be some that don't sell well and need to be liquidated or sold on other channels to help convert the inventory back into some level of working capital.

Amazon has tools to help FBA sellers identify stale inventory, while the non-FBA Amazon seller will need to monitor its inventory by SKU to figure out what might need to be promoted for faster sale.

UNDERSTANDING OF BASIC COST STRUCTURE, INCLUDING OVERHEAD COSTS

Far too many sellers on Amazon understand only the basics of SKU-level profitability, resulting in a blended view of the seller's overall profitability, rather than a pinpoint perspective on which SKUs drive what percentage of profits, while understanding which products are actually costing money to sell on Amazon.

Too many Amazon sellers don't know their profitability until the end of the year when their accountant announces the final numbers, hopefully to the relief of the seller.

It's critical for sellers to understand and compile all of their overhead costs, and recognize that these expenses need to be integrated in some manner into the running total of costs that a seller incurs selling on Amazon.

KNOW WHO IS ALREADY SELLING THE SAME SKUS AS YOU ON AMAZON

Shockingly often, new sellers join Amazon, list their products, and only then discover that the level or type of competition on their listings will make it next to impossible for the new seller to make any sales or any margin.

Before setting up an Amazon seller account, I strongly encourage every seller to spot check its intended catalog on Amazon to see if Amazon Retail is already selling these items.

If so, it's best to walk away from those items right now.

Also, I encourage sellers to gauge what price points are competitive on Amazon, which can often lead to another recognition that the seller can't possibly make any money if it's competing with such low-priced competitors.

KNOW HOW MUCH TIME IS NEEDED TO GET LISTINGS IN PLACE RIGHT AFTER REGISTERED AS AN AMAZON SELLER

Amazon doesn't charge a new seller until the end of the first month on Amazon, during which time, the seller should have created its product offers, and activated at least some with sellable inventory.

If you open your account and don't list your products, you'll still get charged for having your professional seller account open.

Why not plan to invest a bunch of time in the first 30 days to get moving on your account?

Finally, knowing that sales feedback is important to Amazon in gauging the performance of all new sellers, I encourage every new seller to sign up for one of the many inexpensive feedback solicitation tools that send each customer a request for seller feedback.

These include:

- Feedbackgenius.com
- Feedbackfive.com
- Salesbacker.com
- Bqool.com

All of these can all help a seller to get feedback, and show Amazon that the seller is performing well against Amazon's performance criteria while keeping customers happy. Please be aware that Amazon recently changed its terms of services around how feedback and product reviews can be solicited from Amazon customers.

Hence, when selecting such a firm for your seller account, make sure that that firm clearly states that it abides by the new terms of services that Amazon has implemented. From here, you'll want to dig into specific Amazon tactics such as:

- Winning the Buy Box
- Determining your strategy (such as retail arbitrage)
- Selecting the right products

AMAZON SELLING ACCOUNT

Some of the logistics of being a successful Amazon seller should be worked out before you set up the seller account, as you likely won't have as much time to address these after you get started. Use the sheet below to best pre pare before you set up an account.

WHERE DO YOU PLAN TO SEND ORDER RETURNS?

For example, are you going to handle the returns yourself, or send them to a company that specializes in testing/grading returns and making the product available for sale again (e.g., tradeport.com, openedboxreturns.com)?

WHO WILL HANDLE AMAZON CUSTOMER INQUIRIES?

The key is not just having all of the answers, but also respecting Amazon's requirements to respond to all customer inquiries within 24 hours, any day of the year. Hence, figuring out who is on point (with possible backup) is one critical operational issue that should be addressed before opening your Amazon seller account.

If you plan to use Amazon's Fulfillment by Amazon program, decide whether you plan to co-mingle your products with FBA inventory of other sellers of the same products.

☐ Sell through FBA with co-mingle (stickerless)   ☐ Sell through FBA with stickered product

WHAT NAME WILL YOU SELL UNDER ON AMAZON?

While some companies have legitimate reasons to use a different customerfacing name, Amazon is also a place where many sellers purposefully conceal their identity, for reasons that include not wanting brands to know that they are selling online, or the brand is actually the reseller and doesn't want its other retail partners to know it's selling product online direct to consumer.

_____

_____

_____

ARE YOUR PRODUCTS IN CATEGORIES THAT AMAZON HAS GATED? ARE ANY OF YOURS GATED?

Amazon has restrictions on who can sell in certain categories, and while the ungating process is usually surmountable, it's important to recognize that if your desired categories are gated, you will have to apply very quickly to get ungated. Check out Amazon's approval category page before you decide to register on Amazon, and you can learn more about the ungating process, if it applies to your product categories.

_____

_____

_____

Use the checkboxes below to determine how ready your business is from an operational standpoint to sell and succeed on Amazon.

	YES	NO
Do you have good marketing content with which to build product listings (i.e. product images, copy, etc.)	◯	◯
Do you have a clear understanding of your product sourcing avenues? (i.e. If your products sell well on Amazon, do you know how to replenish quickly enough to avoid extensive stockout periods?)	◯	◯
Do you plan on selling the same items over and over? (If yes, you will want to take advantage of Amazon's replenishment alert tools inside Seller Central, as well as other external forecasting tools.)	◯	◯
Do you have a process for identify and addressing stale inventory? (There will always be some product that doesn't sell well, and needs to be liquidated.)	◯	◯
Do you understand the basic cost structure of Amazon, including overhead? (Use the BigCommerce guide to determine your profitability -- Chapter 12.)	◯	◯
Do you know who is already selling the same or similar SKUs as you? (And are those selling well?)	◯	◯
Do you know much time is needed to get listings in place right after registered as an Amazon seller? (You have one month to get up and running moving once you set up the account.)	◯	◯

Now, you're ready to set up. Make sure you have each of these items on hand.

○ Your legal business name, address, and contact information

○ An email address that can be used for this company account. This email account should be set up already, as you will start receiving important emails from Amazon almost immediately.

○ An internationallychargeable credit card with a valid billing address. If the credit card number isn't valid, Amazon will cancel your registration.

○ An email address that can be used for this company account. This email account should be set up already, as you will start receiving important emails from Amazon almost immediately.

○ A phone number where you can be reached during this registration process. Also, have your phone nearby during registration.

○ Your tax identity information, including your Social Security number or your company's Federal Tax ID number. To submit your tax identity information, the registration process will take a brief detour to a "1099-K Tax Document Interview."

○ State tax ID information for states in which you have tax nexus. This physical presence is typically impacted by company offices, warehouses/3PLs, and call centers. If you plan to use Amazon's Fulfillment by Amazon (FBA) program, there may be further tax nexus implications, so we encourage you to talk with a tax attorney or tax accountant who specializes in online seller tax nexus issues (e.g., catchingclouds.net, peisnerjohnson.com) or one of the tax remittance companies that can give you the most current Amazon tax nexus information (e.g., taxjar.com, avalara.com, taxify.co, vertexsmb.com).

06 Amazon Selling Strategies to Get You Started Now

Andrew Tjerlund, Multi-million Dollar Amazon Seller and Amazon Selling Consultant

Too many people are scared to take on, or won't even look at, selling on Amazon as a new way to do business. Before I go any further, let's start here:

Amazon is not going to steal your items.

Amazon buys certain items from me, and their employees pick it up at the factory in China. The items go from "mine" to "Amazon's" as they cross the threshold of the dock doors and into the container. If Amazon doesn't pull the run around in that situation, they are not going to do it to you. The two most common reasons I run into (sans paranoia) for not jumping on Amazon are:

1. Lack of time
2. Channel conflict (i.e. creating a channel that leads to pricing problems across all other distribution channels).

Amazon is viewed as too overwhelming with the kicker that it could disrupt existing ecommerce or traditional sales channels.

This is ludicrous, of course.

As expansive as the Amazon ecosystem is, the decision to sell on Amazon doesn't have to be an all or nothing choice. This same logic would have prevented Columbus from setting sail because he wouldn't have time to map the entire world.

> **True, Amazon can be a lot of work, but do it right and it's clear sailing.**

It's also worth mentioning that **if your brand is of any decent size, the reality is that someone will be selling your brand on Amazon anyway.** The question for most brands is not whether they will have an Amazon presence, but rather what sort of presence will they have to protect their brand.

So, let's dive into your options.

Cost and Time Effective Strategies for Selling on Amazon

DIP IN JUST YOUR TOE

No one says you have to offer all your products on Amazon. Familiarize yourself with Amazon by just putting up a few products to start. Putting up a few products at the get-go allows you to learn some of the administrative processes so you can ultimately streamline or eliminate them.

It is likely you are coordinating Amazon with outside systems, training people for these new activities or going through an Amazon specific process for the first time. Give yourself a chance to be successful by understanding what you are doing before you try to improve it.

For anyone still not sold on diversifying to Amazon, remember this: **the reality is that your competitors are already selling on Amazon.**

How do you make sure your brand is part of the Amazon customer consideration set? If you're not there, your competitors are eating up Amazon customer demand -- more than 200MM active custom-ers and over $100B of sales annually. It's worth it to have even a few products on there as an additional sales channel.

THE FOLDING CHAIRS AND TABLES EXAMPLE

A great example of this "just dip your toe in" approach is the online store Folding Chairs and Tables. They sell custom folding chairs and tables, and launched on Amazon with 1 product before the holiday in 2016 — a bundled chair and table package of their website best sellers. They sold out and ended up having to remove their Amazon listings for a period of time due to the high orders.

Over time, they were able to restock at appropriate levels factoring in the added volume from Amazon and now are having great success on Amazon and their webstore across a variety of SKUs.

This is the benefit of going slow -- you can pull down, readjust back office and manufacturing needs and then get back up, running and making money FAST.

REINVENT YOUR BRAND FOR AMAZON

If conflict and time are a concern, another strategy is to sell your products under a new brand name. They can be the identical items, bundles or variations available only on Amazon. This allows you to gain access to Amazon's huge customer base and try different prices or packages without affecting your standard products and established brand.

Plus, you can put up these items without worrying about how it affects your entire catalog, which should speed up any internal approval process.

"Amazon Only" brands give you new freedoms to cater to specific markets and is an excellent way to test for new products.

Let's take a closer look at that Folding Chairs and Tables example -- notice how all items they are selling on Amazon are sets, or bundled?

This is not how they sell on their main site.

Instead, on Amazon, they sell bundled chair and table sets -- while on their web store, they sell individual items (often at bulk for B2B) with financing options.

Two strategies -- two strong revenue channels.

MAKE OTHERS DO THE WORK

Expedited shipping, feedback, ratings, optimization and sponsored search are often new frontiers to your business. These are all legitimate and demand a new Amazon seller's attention, but wonderfully there are many solutions to these problems.

Outsourcing these activities that are highly unlikely to be your strength is not only affordable but also quite effective.

Thousands of Amazon professionals are available for $3-$10 per hour.

In the same way, Amazon lets you outsource the promotion and customer acquisition of your products, services like Freeeup, Upwork and Lancer let you outsource the activities that are unique to the Amazon marketplace.

No one knows the business better than the business itself.

Joining Amazon can be intimidating, but by sculpting how one enters the Amazon marketplace in a way that fits your goals and company structure, it can be done with limited risk.

Once the business is up and running, many programs can be used to simplify the selling process.

Your Options (and Advice) for Exactly How You Sell on Amazon

> **Amazon is a shopping site the same way a Swiss Army Knife is a knife. If you utilize it strictly at its basic level, you are missing 95% of its value.**

Think big when it comes to selling on Amazon and your desired success. You can make a bunch of money on Amazon with a lot less work by setting up your selling method correctly.

Here is how.

FULFILLED BY MERCHANT LISTING

Short and Sweet

Fulfilled by Merchant is the basic Amazon listing. ou create or jump on an existing listing for a product on Amazon, manage all customer service and take care of all the picking, packing, shipping, and returns.

When to Use It

Use the Fulfilled by Merchant option as little as possible as your primary listing. It is alright to keep a merchant fulfilled listing active as a backup for your inventory at Amazon's fulfillment centers in case of stock outs, but that should be it.

These offers carry the least weight in Amazon's search algorithm. These are most often appropriate for really low-velocity sellers or super high-cost items you simply can't afford to inventory.

Real Example of How to Do it Wrong

If any of your best products are fulfilled by merchant, especially in competitive categories, you are doing it wrong. If you want to see examples of these listings, simply submit a search of any product to Amazon and then dig to page 20 and beyond.

Do you think it is just coincidence that you don't see any items available as Prime this deep in the results?

Real Example of How to Do it Right

Below is the top selling outdoor ice maker on Amazon. Note three important things:

1. it doesn't sell often
2. it's expensive
3. it's heavy.

This is the appropriate use of fulfilled by merchant (FBM).

First, for it to be the best seller in a category and only have five reviews, that indicates that it's not a major mover. This and factor number two: **it's price tag.**

It may not make sense to stock a bunch of these and warehouse them at Amazon. Why not drop ship them from the manufacturer once you get the sale and cash in simply by putting up a listing on Amazon? That's likely what is being done.

Lastly, at 129 lbs, having it sent to you, then to Amazon, then to the customer may make any other method cost prohibitive.

FULFILLED BY AMAZON LISTING

Short and Sweet

This is the more evolved version of the typical Amazon listing. You are still the seller, but you send inventory to Amazon's fulfillment centers.

Now, when an item sells, Amazon automatically picks, packs and ships your items to the buyers (for a fee). Plus, they handle all basic customer service tasks such as tracking and returns. Using this method makes your items Prime eligible, and **Prime users are Amazon's most valuable customers as they buy more regularly and spend more.** Having your items in FBA is also attractive to Amazon's search algorithm, helping your product be seen more often by more people.

When to Use It

Use this method when you want to simplify the process of selling online and also maintain full control over the product listing information and price.

This is particularly important for sellers needing to maintain MAP pricing because you set the price.

Real Example of How to Do it Wrong

The seller Blue Monster has decided to purchase inventory and pay to send it into Amazon. This must be with the hope that buyers who trust the brand enough to choose to shop on Amazon will choose to pay more to avoid buying from Amazon.

Does that make any sense? These items will sit until their expiration day.

Real Example of How to Do it Right

If a buyer were to click "Add to Cart" for this item, they would buy from "Professional Grade Products" for $499. Note that as shown in the second image, this same item can be purchased for $399 (plus a little shipping) from a different seller. So, why does Amazon promote the $499 offer and make it the default choice for customers?

Because it is Fulfilled by Amazon.

Amazon's algorithm gives massive positive clout to items fulfilled by Amazon. In this case, it thinks the Prime offer is a better overall value to the customer, even though it costs $85 more. If there were no Prime offer, "Northern Tool" would almost certainly win the Buy Box every time.

However, by using fulfillment by Amazon, another seller has been able to increase both their sales volume and margin.

VENDOR EXPRESS/VENDOR CENTRAL

Short and Sweet

You are not selling on Amazon anymore; you are selling to Amazon. Amazon Retail is voraciously acquiring access to more products, and they want to buy products from you and sell those items themselves (they choose the end price).

The following are simply myths:

1. Amazon will "steal" your product.
2. Selling to Amazon lowers your margin.
3. Amazon is a difficult partner.
4. A fairy comes at night to collect your lost teeth.

Fact: Amazon owns its platform. **Why fight it when they want you to join the team?** Anybody can sign up for Vendor Express. Vendor Central is invite-only. The main difference is you get a human buyer with Vendor Central.

When to Use It

If you want to leverage the growing customer base of Amazon without having an Amazon segment of your business, this is the way to go. They act, for the most part, like any stocking customer. Selling to Amazon can minimize or eliminate the need to forecast, stock, or handle customer service for your products.

Real Example of How to Do it Wrong

Common complaints from my clients about selling to Amazon come down to the setup. If you do this right, you should not have any issues.

First, some people are just overwhelmed by the large amount of information they need to provide to Amazon to set up a product. However, it is not much different than what you would include in an online store, so although it may take a lot of time for those with large catalogs, it is not hard.

Second, some complain that Amazon orders in too small of quantities or buys at too low of a price.

This just makes me shake my head.

During the setup, you select or approve the price and the case pack of minimum order quantities. If you don't like them, that's on you. Plus, they can be edited, so just fix it.

Real Example of How to Do it Right

Typically, to increase sales volumes, a seller would have to lower their price – and thus their margins – to win more sales. However, this seller can maximize margin and still have their items sell at the lowest price, ensuring sales velocity.

In the first example, the seller of this item is selling these furnace filters to Amazon for $31.44*, with Amazon paying all shipping costs, eating any returns and spending money promoting this listing. So, yes, Amazon is selling the item for about 20% below cost, plus covering all those related fees.

What a deal, right?

For many products, Amazon is fine with losing money on every sale to gain traction on the internet at large, gain scale logistics and help drive long-term traffic to these products. Meanwhile, you can cash in by having your cake (margin) and eating it too (sales velocity).

*Trust me.

DROPSHIP CENTRAL

Short and Sweet

Think Vendor Central, but where you still pick, pack and ship the item once Amazon sells it. **It is not available to everybody, even those with Vendor Central accounts.** However, since this book likely has the longevity of the Dead Sea Scrolls, I figured I should mention it for when your great grandchildren read this.

When to Use It

If an item is expensive and sells only once or twice per year or is physically too large to ship twice, this can be a useful method. You gain the Prime designation, have to build/order the items only once Amazon has already sold it and you gain the SEO boost Amazon gives to the products it sells directly.

Real Example of How to Do it Wrong

The only way to mess this up is to tell Amazon you can drop ship a product you don't have or can't build in time. If you don't have it, tell them.

Real Example of How to Do it Right

Can you blame Amazon for not wanting to stock industrial freezer cases? However, they do sell them (you can even see that this has two happy reviews).

This item is likely sold by Amazon through Drop Ship Central.

Amazon gets the sale, allows a few weeks for the item to get built and then the item is shipped one time directly to the customer (note that the item is still considered Prime despite the delivery time of up to 5 weeks). This means the manufacturer can focus on building large freezers and leave all the Amazon shenanigans to Amazon themselves.

The Amazon Cocktail

See these examples of sellers mixing methods to create savory sales.

FBM AND VC COCKTAIL

Corentium makes this product and sells directly on Amazon through FBM. However, they also sell directly to Amazon.

Although most sales will likely go to Amazon, by creating what the algorithm sees as a competitive listing, Corentium is not only keeping Amazon's markup in check, but also has a backup listing in case Amazon stocks out. Get all of the optimization gains by selling directly to Amazon and still not be dependent on Amazon to get the stock or price the product appropriately.

FBA AND OFF AMAZON COCKTAIL

Selling using FBA can be intimidating for sellers for many reasons, partly because they feel that they no longer have direct access to their inventory. They want to benefit from the ease and SEO boost that comes with using FBA, but still need inventory to fulfill orders from other sources.

What they often overlook is that if you sell via FBA, you still own the inventory at Amazon's fulfillment centers. In fact, **you can have Amazon pick, pack and ship orders for sales that were made outside of Amazon.**

For example, this seller keeps all their inventory at Amazon's fulfillment centers and still sells on eBay. All order information from eBay sales are submitted to Amazon and then Amazon picks, packs, and ships these paddles to the eBay customers. In this case, using FBA not only helps sales on Amazon but makes selling on eBay less of a hassle.

Editor's note: eBay is shutting down a lot of these Amazon-fulfilled orders going to eBay customers, as the shipper may appear as "Amazon Fulfillment" which triggers eBay turning off sellers' elite status within eBay. We'll update this content as those changes are made or services shut down.

THE LONG ISLAND

Want to try to gain the combined benefits of FBM (constant stock), FBA (Prime with price control) and selling to Amazon (maximum exposure and customer trust)?

It is more to manage, but this seller uses all three methods to try to maximize sales regardless of the administrative hassle.

As the brand owner, Hayabusa is selling Mixed Martial Art Gloves themselves through an FBM listing. They are also selling to a reseller using FBA and directly to Amazon.

Managing their all of these methods can be quite the task, but it is possible and can be effective.

Editor's note: This strategy doesn't work for all brands. The purpose of this chapter is to outline as many Amazon options as possible to prove that you have multiple ways you can use the marketplace. According to James Thomson, the founder of the PROSPER Show, "This is a recipe for price wars and rarely does the brand win when it's selling to Amazon while creating competition through another 3P seller." The example above proves that it can work, but it doesn't always.

Wrapping Everything Together

Overall, think about how you want the Amazon channel to fit within your existing business and choose a method that works for you. It is easiest to start with one method and then incorporate others later.

Consider which administrative activities you can manage effectively and easily and which you would like to avoid.

There is not one right answer, but keep in mind that **most items that go from FBM to FBA see a 10%-20% increase in sales and a boost of 40%-50% once they are sold directly to Amazon.**

07 Amazon Selling Pitfalls Even the Savviest Sellers Forget [Infographic]

James Thomson, PROSPER Show Founder

So you're up and running as an Amazon seller, and you think you've figured out the Amazon marketplace. The good news is, if you've made it out alive (and profitably) through your first holiday shopping season, you're doing well. But, there are a number of issues that even large or long-term Amazon sellers don't figure out.

Selling on Amazon is endlessly complex, with traps that even veterans fall into.

I'm pleased to unveil the pitfalls to you now –– but like a child who thinks she's figured out how a magician does a trick, you still will need to work hard to avoid the common problems many sellers encounter when they start selling on Amazon.

Knowing these will at least set you up to be more aware of where those pitfalls might be hiding. Use the infographic to help visualize the issues and read through exactly how to solve them in the article below.

TIPS AND TRICKS FOR SUCCEEDING ON

AMAZON FROM DAY ONE

Amazon is a different beast than your own website. Find the most common pitfalls below and exactly how you can avoid the drop.

TOP-LEVEL AMAZON PITFALLS

% TAX SETUP

WHAT YOU NEED TO KNOW

The responsibility of remitting tax is not optional. The seller ultimately has the responsibility of paying its taxes.

WHAT YOU NEED TO DO NOW

Go into the Settings –> Tax Settings, and designate not only in which states you want Amazon to collect state sales tax, but also set the "Use default Product Tax Code" setting to "A_GEN_TAX."

WHAT OFTEN HAPPENS

Amazon's default when setting up new listings is to designate each SKU as having a notax label, which can overwrite the seller's general request to collect state sales tax across all of its catalog.

ONE LAST HICCUP

Selling via FBA? All FBA sellers should invest in a tax consultation with an online seller tax consultant in order to understand the responsibilities and potential liabilities of using FBA.

⏸ PROFITABILITY

WHAT YOU NEED TO KNOW

There isn't much long-term benefit to being a big, but not particularly profitable seller on Amazon.

WHAT YOU NEED TO DO NOW

Get a SKU-level understanding of profitability, incorporating overhead and indirect costs into each SKU's profit calculation.

WHAT OFTEN HAPPENS

Too many sellers focus on topline sales numbers rather than bottom line profits.

ONE LAST HICCUP

Don't forget about certain less than obvious Amazon fees, and product write downs/write-offs.

FBA PITFALLS

CO-MINGLED, STICKERLESS SKUS

WHAT YOU NEED TO KNOW

A seller has the option of sending product into FBA without having to provide SKU-level stickers on each unit.

WHAT YOU NEED TO DO NOW

At roughly $0.20/unit for Amazon to sticker items, the costs of stickering FBA units is far lower than the implied cost of having a seller account suspended for apparently selling counterfeit co-mingled product to a customer.

WHAT OFTEN HAPPENS

Stickerless inventory has the potential to get mixed in with the inventory of other FBA sellers of the same SKU.

ONE LAST HICCUP

You read that right, you can get kicked off Amazon for selling counterfeit product that didn't even come from you. Sticker your products.

SETTING UP STICKERED SKUS

WHAT YOU NEED TO KNOW

By default, each new FBA account starts off as stickerless.

WHAT YOU NEED TO DO NOW

GChange the default setting before creating your first shipment to FBA per SKU.

WHAT OFTEN HAPPENS

Too many sellers focus on topline sales numbers rather than bottom line profits..

ONE LAST HICCUP

Otherwise, you will have to create a duplicate stickered offer on the same product listing.

REPACKAGE UNSELLABLE CUSTOMER RETURNS

WHAT YOU NEED TO KNOW

Amazon defaults every FBA seller's account to be enabled for "Repackage Unsellable Customer Returns." This means when a customer returns an FBA order, if that product's packaging has been damaged, Amazon may apply its own packaging in an effort to make the unit resellable.

WHAT YOU NEED TO DO NOW

Turn off this repackaging feature immediately, and handle all repackaging yourself in order to ensure only the highest quality product.

WHAT OFTEN HAPPENS

It's not unusual for customers to see this Amazon repackaging as potentially an identifier of counterfeit or used product, resulting in a customer complaint or even an infringement against the seller for apparently selling used condition product as new condition product.

ONE LAST HICCUP

Keep this turned on if your product is sold in a generic polybag or generic cardboard box (with no logos on the packaging) -- it's easier.

OPERATIONAL PITFALLS

RETURNS

WHAT YOU NEED TO KNOW

Returned products aren't likely to be 100% recoverable as new condition products.

WHAT YOU NEED TO DO NOW

Track the recovery rate of each SKU and which products are most likely to be returned damaged by customers, and you can identify which products you need to remove from your active catalog. You'll also identify with which products and brands you may need to negotiate a returns allowance with your suppliers.

WHAT OFTEN HAPPENS

For too many sellers, handling returns is something done at the end of month when they have time.

ONE LAST HICCUP

You may be surprised to discover just how much financial loss you incur because of high return rates and high write-down/write-off costs.

DUPLICATE LISTINGS FROM COMPETITORS

WHAT YOU NEED TO KNOW

Duplicate listings on Amazon can be an effective way for competitors to divert traffic away from your product listings back to theirs.

WHAT YOU NEED TO DO NOW

It's worth, at least once a quarter, to search the whole Amazon catalog for duplicate listings of your items.

WHAT OFTEN HAPPENS

Sellers don't pay attention or ever do a search for duplicate listings.

ONE LAST HICCUP

If you find other listings of the same products, consider filing tickets with Seller Support to get duplicate listings merged together. And, if the duplicate listings were created maliciously by sellers using incorrect data, it may be worth also filing tickets reporting violations against those sellers.

PRICING AND PROCUREMENT

WHAT YOU NEED TO KNOW

It's only a matter of time before some competitor with a lower margin threshold starts selling the same product, and basically makes your offers unsellable.

WHAT YOU NEED TO DO NOW

Sellers should, at least once a month, focus a few days on procurement of new selection, as some portion of their existing catalog will likely become unprofitable or below an acceptable margin threshold, leading to a need for better use of capital on other product selection.

WHAT OFTEN HAPPENS

Too many sellers be slow to plan how to evolve their catalogs over the next three to six months.

ONE LAST HICCUP

The active catalog you have today isn't likely to be as profitable or relevant in 6 to 12 months from now.

LISTING OPTIMIZATIONS

For many sellers, the process of building and optimizing listings is a one-time deal, as they understandably turn their focus to other operational matters.

USE SPONSORED PRODUCT AD CAMPAIGN REPORT

In this, you can see the exact keywords connected to Amazon customers actually buying your products. Use this to optimize your listings for Amazon SEO.

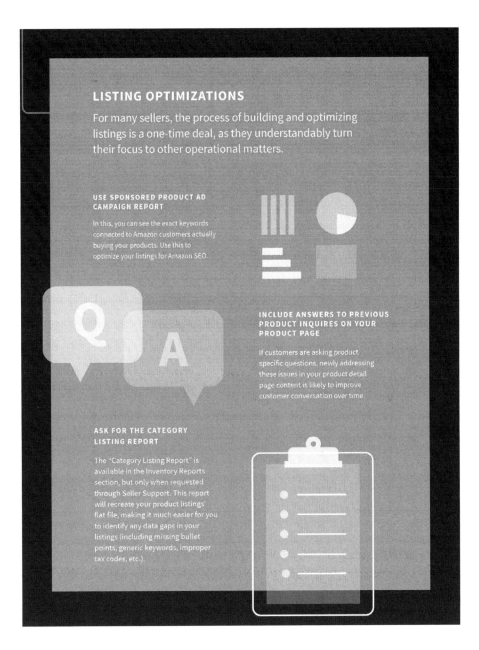

INCLUDE ANSWERS TO PREVIOUS PRODUCT INQUIRES ON YOUR PRODUCT PAGE

If customers are asking product specific questions, newly addressing these issues in your product detail page content is likely to improve customer conversation over time.

ASK FOR THE CATEGORY LISTING REPORT

The "Category Listing Report" is available in the Inventory Reports section, but only when requested through Seller Support. This report will recreate your product listings' flat file, making it much easier for you to identify any data gaps in your listings (including missing bullet points, generic keywords, improper tax codes, etc.).

Tax Setup

It's a little shocking how many sellers never set up state tax collection options on Amazon, thinking that Amazon somehow automatically takes care of all sales tax issues from sales on the Amazon marketplace.

It turns out nothing could be further from the truth.

While Amazon is happy to collect state sales tax for you (for a small fee), **it's up to every seller to indicate in which states it wants Amazon to collect tax,** and to manage the remittance of the taxes to the appropriate tax jurisdictions across the country.

There are many tax remittance services available for online sellers (such as taxjar.com, avalara.com, taxify.com, and vertexsmb.com), but the seller ultimately has the responsibility of paying its taxes.

While a seller may choose not to collect state sales tax (choosing to absorb that as a cost of doing business), the responsibility of remitting the tax is not optional.

A seller can designate its account to collect state sales tax in particular states.

Unfortunately, however, **Amazon's default when setting up new listings is to designate each SKU as having a no-tax label,** which can overwrite the seller's general request to collect state sales tax across all of its catalog.

SET YOUR TAXES UP RIGHT THE FIRST GO AROUND

My advice is to, immediately upon signing up a new seller account, go into the **Settings -> Tax Settings,** and designate not only in which states you want Amazon to collect state sales tax, but also set the "Use default Product Tax Code" setting to "A_GEN_TAX."

Amazon typically defaults to A_GEN_NOTAX, where no tax is being collected.

While the seller may offer products that warrant a slightly different tax rate, that level of tweaking can follow later.

If the seller is using Fulfillment by Amazon (FBA) and isn't proactively collecting state sales tax in all of the tax-collecting states where Amazon has fulfillment centers, it won't be long before the seller accumulates tax liability from having incurred tax nexus by way of FBA inventory being stored – even briefly – in these states' fulfillment warehouses.

Each FBA seller should invest in a tax consultation with an online seller tax consultant to understand the responsibilities and potential liabilities of using FBA.

Profitability

Too many sellers focus on top line sales numbers rather than bottom line profits.

> *"I want to sell $1MM/year on Amazon" or "If only I could get to be a $10MM/year seller on Amazon."*

Honestly, other than ego and maybe a few volume discounts, there isn't much long-term benefit to being a big, but not particularly profitable seller on Amazon.

FOCUS ON BOTTOM GROWTH AND ACCOUNT FOR ALL COSTS UPFRONT

I'd much rather see any seller grow its bottom line profits year-over-year much faster than its top line sales. That typically requires a SKU-level understanding of profitability, incorporating overhead and indirect costs into each SKU's profit calculation.

This includes certain less than obvious Amazon fees, and product write-downs/write-offs. While I'll discuss this matter much more in a subsequent chapter, it's important to focus on those parts of your catalog that make you money and shed those parts that don't make you money.

> **Stop averaging everything out, and looking only at your overall sales numbers and margins.**

Start thinking about every SKU you sell on Amazon as having its own P&L, its own market forces, and its own level and types of competitions.

Such an approach has helped many a seller rationalize its catalog, focusing on bottom line growth ahead of all other financial goals.

Fulfillment by Amazon

THE ISSUE WITH CO-MINGLED SKUS

There are a number of problems here, and I'll start with the use of co-mingled "stickerless" SKUs.

As mentioned in a previous chapter, a seller has the option of sending product into FBA without having to provide SKU-level stickers on each unit.

Such stickerless inventory has the potential to get mixed in with the inventory of other FBA sellers of the same SKU.

Then when a customer places an order from one FBA seller, Amazon pulls the most convenient inventory, even if that inventory isn't actually the inventory that the seller sent into FBA itself.

And, if other sellers have sent in counterfeit product or used condition product that they are trying to pawn off as new condition product, now the seller with this new sale may get itself into trouble with Amazon for selling problematic product to a customer.

> **Amazon responds when customers complain about product quality -- and the heavy lifting falls on the individual sale-level brand.**

At roughly $0.20/unit for Amazon to sticker items or whatever a seller's own warehouse costs are, we see the costs of stickering FBA units as far lower than the implied cost of having one's seller account suspended for apparently selling counterfeit co-mingled product to a customer.

STICKERLESS V. STICKERED INVENTORY

The other complicated issue around stickerless vs. stickered FBA inventory is when a seller designates its account to be stickered.

> **By default, each new FBA account starts off as stickerless.**

When a seller creates a shipment of product to send to Amazon's fulfillment centers, that stickerless designation will be applied to the seller's SKUs and will remain forever going forward with that SKU.

So, if the seller wants it's FBA product to be stickered, the seller has to change the default setting before creating its first shipment to FBA. Otherwise, the seller will have to create a duplicate stickered offer on the same product listing.

We've seen many sellers not get this sequencing right, leading to situations where they think they changed their account to stickered, only to discover that certain SKUs remain stickerless because they were initially sent to FBA before the whole account got switched over to stickered.

So if in doubt, flip everything to stickered (not co-mingled) immediately upon turning on FBA (but before creating the first FBA shipment). Or. contact Amazon Seller Support to get clarification if any SKUs in your catalog are unknowingly stickerless.

Bottom line: when you start off, make sure you read up on how to sell on Amazon FBA so you don't fall victim to these pitfalls.

REPACKAGE UNSELLABLE CUSTOMER RETURNS

Next, Amazon defaults every FBA seller's account to enabled for "Repackage Unsellable Customer Returns."

This means when a customer returns an FBA order, if that product's packaging is damaged, Amazon may apply its own packaging to make the unit resellable.

Unfortunately, it's not unusual for customers to see this Amazon repackaging as potentially an identifier of counterfeit or used product, resulting in a customer complaint or even an infringement against the seller for selling used condition product as new condition product.

Unless you sell your product in a generic polybag or generic cardboard box (with no logos on the packaging), **I suggest turning off this repackaging feature immediately, and handling all repackaging yourself to ensure only the highest quality product** (with proper packaging) is presented to Amazon customers.

Listing Optimization

There are a number of sources of data available within Seller Central that can be used to improve the listing quality of your catalog.

For many sellers, the process of building and optimizing listings is a one-time deal, as they understandably turn their focus to other operational matters.

USE THE SPONSORED PRODUCT AD CAMPAIGN REPORTS

A significant opportunity, however, lies in using the reports from the Sponsored Product ad campaigns.

In these reports, you can see the exact keywords that were connected to Amazon customers buying your products.

By examining these reports periodically (specifically for automatic targeting campaigns), you'll find that there are keywords leading to sales that you never anticipated being effective. Lifting those terms directly into your generic keywords will improve the SEO discoverability of your listings.

I encourage sellers to repeat this process every three months to make sure that customers' behavior specific to certain words haven't changed.

And with the generic keyword capacity for words now much larger than ever before, there is room to add many more keywords and get click benefit through SEO rather than paid efforts.
Include answers to previous product inquiries on your product page
It's also worth paying special attention the inquiries that you get from Amazon customers.

If customers are asking product specific questions, newly addressing these issues in your product detail page content is likely to improve customer conversation over time.

For too many Amazon sellers, the customer inquiry process doesn't include an indexing of questions and answers back to specific SKUs, thereby causing a seller to lose out on known product clarifications or embellishments that are needed.

ASK FOR THE CATEGORY LISTING REPORT

Finally, I'm a big fan of the "Category Listing Report," a report available in the Inventory Reports section, but only when requested through Seller Support.

This report will recreate your product listings' flat file, making it much easier for you to identify any data gaps in your listings (including missing bullet points, generic keywords, improper tax codes, etc.).

While you request this report for only a finite period (i.e., seven days, 30 days), it's worth pulling this report at least quarterly to make sure your product listings contain all of the necessary data you believe they should.

Operations

And now the biggest category of all. Managing the operations of an Amazon seller business is the most time-consuming part of every seller's day. Too many sellers don't focus on the right activities, leading them to work too hard to make Amazon money.

Do you have a clear process for handling returns efficiently?

Do you have a way of testing or grading returns, upgrading packaging where needed, and recovering as much revenue as possible by making these items sellable again on Amazon (or some other channel, as needed)?

For too many sellers, handling returns is something done at the end of the month when they have time, rather than something that is managed strategically through analytics and continuous improvement.

Yes, returned products aren't likely to be 100% recoverable as new condition products.

However, if you carefully track the return rate of each SKU, the recovery rate of each SKU (i.e., what proportion of expected new condition revenue you actually recover from each SKU), and which products are most likely to be returned damaged by customers, you can identify which products you need to remove from your active catalog.

You'll also identify with which products and brands you may need to negotiate a returns allowance with your suppliers/distributors/brands.

Once you have this data in hand, you'll likely be surprised to discover just how much financial loss you incur because of high return rates and high write-down/write-off costs.

Some of the best sellers on Amazon know, for each SKU, exactly where to sell returned products to get the highest recovery rate.

It's worth talking with other sellers to figure out if you are unknowingly leaving a lot of money on the table by mishandling returned products, or if you are appropriately managing returned products as a core part of your overall seller business.

LOOK OUT FOR DUPLICATE LISTINGS FROM COMPETITORS

Duplicate listings on Amazon can be an effective way for competitors to divert traffic away from your product listings back to theirs.

> **It's worth, at least once a quarter, to search the whole Amazon catalog for duplicate listings of your items.**

If you find other listings of the same products, consider filing tickets with Seller Support to get duplicate listings merged. And, if the duplicate listings were created maliciously by sellers using incorrect data (e.g., irrelevant UPCs or incorrect brand names), it may be worth also filing tickets reporting violations against those sellers. I have seen far too many sellers confused about why their sales are dropping on top-selling items, only to find that the sales are being diverted to a duplicate listing newly created by a coy competitor.

INVENTORY MANAGEMENT SKILLS ARE REQUIRED

Inventory management skills require constant refinement on Amazon, whether it's actively addressing soon-to-be stale inventory or rebalancing products based on changing customer preferences.

> **While I see most sellers ramping up inventory levels for the holiday shopping season, few sellers stock up enough products to cover most of January as well.**

Often this leads to unnecessary stock-outs caused by higher than expected demand in December or inadequate time to replenish in early January when your suppliers are closed for the holidays.

Either way, I like to see sellers planning their holiday shopping inventory levels in such a way that they potentially overstock a little bit for January and February, thereby giving themselves a little bit of breathing room in December, January, and February. Such an approach is especially relevant for products that are expected to continue to have some meaningful sales after December.

Test-buy Your Competitors

Test-buying your competitors' products on Amazon is a very easy way to figure out what your competitors are up to, regarding how they package product, how they follow up through email to customers, and how they handle customer returns (if needed). While you and your competitors may be selling the same products, there are likely some aspects of your competitors' overall offering that you can learn through periodic test buys.

Plan for Pricing and Procurement

Finally, with so many changes to competitors and prices on Amazon, I have watched too many sellers be slow to plan how to evolve their catalogs over the next three to six months.

Sellers should, at least once a month, focus a few days on the procurement of new selection, as some portion of their existing catalog will likely become unprofitable or below an acceptable margin threshold, leading to a need for better use of capital on other product selection. This is particularly the case for resellers that don't have exclusive sourcing relationships.

> **It's only a matter of time before some competitor with a lower margin threshold starts selling the same product, and makes your offers unsellable.**

While a brand may think it has decent control of its distribution, Amazon is a very efficient marketplace for gray-market or diverted product to surface, leading you to find that you have to cut your prices just to match some new entrant. For private label sellers on Amazon, remember that that your product sales successes on Amazon are an invitation for the next private label seller to copy your product and make a lower priced version; so keep evolving and stay nimble.

> **The active catalog you have today isn't likely to be as profitable or relevant in 6 to 12 months from now.**

08

How One Pillow Manufacturer Is Putting Amazon Fraudsters to Bed, One Scammer at a Time

Amanda Horner, CEO, CNH Pillow

In 1990, my dad set up shop with my mom, selling this pillow with a hole in the middle. He's a derma-tologist, and made the pillow to provide relief to patients of his suffering from tender ears caused by a condition called Chondrodermatitis Nodularis Helicis (CNH for short).

They've been in business ever since then, and up until this year when my husband and I bought the business from them, they did everything exactly the same as they did back in 1990. That means no advertising, marketing or sales channel changes in almost 30 years.

So, my husband I took over in January and have since changed everything (it is 2017, after all!)We updated our website and joined BigCommerce in January of 2017. From there, we put ads on Google. Then, a few months ago, we started selling on Amazon.

That's when our sales doubled!

My parents were shocked. "That's the power of Amazon!" I told them. We were going to be the next big Amazon success story –– I just knew it.

And then, our listing was deactivated. Someone else had the lowest price.

"OK,' I said to my husband, "that's impossible. Nobody else can have the lowest price for this pillow, because nobody else has this pillow. My dad invented it. We have the lowest price, because we have the only price."

I was freaking out. It was the first time either of us had ever experienced fraud — and I had no idea what was going on.

But that was then.

I've since learned that the kind of fraud we were subject to is a huge problem on Amazon. I've also gone through all the necessary steps each and every time to make it stop. And for my business, I have it down to a science.

Let's start with what not to do.

What Happens When You Call Amazon About a Fraudulent Seller?

After that first incident, in my panic mode, I called Amazon customer service. At that point, I had tried to do everything I could within seller central. Nothing was working. So, I picked up the phone. They wouldn't tell me anything about the other seller.

I supposed that it made sense, after all, it's private and it could be "somebody else's business," in theory. But we're the only ones who make this pillow, remember?

So I told Amazon, "This person says they're selling my product and they can't be! Nobody else has my product. It's my own product. Nobody has it."

To be fair, they were very calm about the whole thing and let me freak out over the phone. They asked me to explain the issue entirely -- and that they'd look into it. So, I did.

Here's what I told them:
- Another seller listed my item
- They used my picture with my hand on the pillow
- They used the description that I wrote myself
- They had *our* customer service number on there
- And worst of all, they lowered the price to $5.47 -- when the cost is $59.95.

Let's get transparent on the pricing part. Our pillow costs us $20-something to make it. There's no way somebody could have made a similar or knockoff product for even close to $5.

Of course, they weren't saying it was a knockoff. They were saying it was the real deal. Our product. Our custom-made, copyrighted product. It was frightening, but Amazon was able to take that seller down decently quickly. Problem solved, right? Wrong.

As soon as that seller was taken down, a few hours later another one popped right up again. It's part of the scam.

Beware the Amazon Seller Scam

Several years ago, Amazon had a big push to become a global marketplace, and so they opened themselves up and made it super easy for international groups or people to sell and open up a store on the platform. Essentially, almost anybody, almost anywhere, can sell on Amazon within minutes.

It goes like this...

One scammer somewhere in the world says to a want-to-be Amazon merchant:

> *"Pay us a certain amount of money, and we'll set you up with a store on Amazon. You pay us and we'll set you up with a store with 20,000 items for sale. People buy the items from you, and all you have to do is drop ship. You never actually hold any items in stock at all."*

Now, I can only assume that somebody has a program which allows a "seller" to select many items at once and set a price that's some very low percentage of the price that is originally on there. It's why our $59.95 pillow was listed at a little over $5.

I say that this is the case because when you go to the storefronts of these fraudulent sellers, they have hundreds, if not thousands of products listed, all at insanely low prices.

The products they list alongside might be related, or not. In our case, there was the CNH pillow, plus a lot of other bedding, and then a lot random stuff.

It's almost always the case, however, that the scammers will target 'Just Launched' items, from genuine sellers with few or no ratings. This has something to do with the way Amazon lists products.

If I'm a new seller (a genuine one) with no reviews, and I'm 'competing' as it were with two scammers, listing my product for a fraction of the price, then even though none of us has any reviews, the scammers will appear above me because their offering is less expensive.

Why Does the Scam Work In the First Place?

The scam works in part purely because of the sheer size of the Amazon marketplace. Even if Amazon had a team dedicated to tracking down the scammers, it would be incredibly difficult to catch them all at launch.

In practice, the scam works because before shoppers buy one of these fake items, they're told it will ship from inside the U.S. Then, as soon as they place the order, the fake seller changes the shipping information from U.S. Post, to China Post, and attaches a tracking number.

How do they attach a tracking number when there's no product to send? Yep, it's fake, too.

Why put a tracking number in the first place? Amazon pays sellers every two weeks. Items posted from China take between three and four weeks to arrive. The plan is that they'll get paid in two weeks, then, when in four weeks time the customer hasn't received their item, that customer will complain to Amazon.

The customer will be refunded by Amazon, but by then, the fake seller has already been removed, and set up shop as somebody completely different. Even if they succeed in getting a small fraction of those sales to work, the scammers are making money. The customer wastes time, but they eventually get their money back.

In the end, it's the seller who's losing out, because the customers are angry, trust is broken and they might never want to buy from you again. This has been the case with us a few times, and when I speak to customers who have been scammed, the conversation goes something like this:

> *"Hey, I haven't received my order."*
> *"I'm sorry. I have no record of you buying from us."*
> *"I only paid $7.00"*

And so I explain what's happened, and usually they say, "Well, that sucks. Can I order now?"
But it's a waste of everyone's time.

Is There Anything Amazon Can Do to Fix This?

Probably. Making sellers jump through a few more hoops before being able to list items would be a start. And placing some restrictions on new sellers would help to curb the scammers, or at least slow them down.

But honestly, the way we've dealt with things on our own has been really effective, and if it can save you the hassle of going through what we went through, then I would be all too happy to share.

How to Stop the Amazon Scammers

There's a bit of policing you'll need to do yourself when it comes to taking down the scammers, but it's totally worth it.

KEEP CHECKING YOUR INVENTORY

If you have just a few items for sale on Amazon, then the first thing you ought to do is go to your inventory page on a daily basis — I do this multiple times a day — to make sure you've got the lowest price.

I've got my pillow, and I've got my extra pillow cover. Those are my only two items. So I know that I should have the only price on Amazon.

There's a little green check mark by each item saying, "Yes, you've got the lowest price." I know if that's the case, I'm fine. If you no longer have the lowest price, and you're the only one selling that item, there could be problem. If somebody has significantly undercut you on a similar item, do some research before going in guns blazing.

GET AS MANY REVIEWS AS POSSIBLE

If your product has lots of positive reviews, it will help to keep you up high in the listings. It's also more work for scammers to fake reviews right after launch.

BE OPEN AND HONEST IN YOUR PRODUCT DESCRIPTION

The other thing I do — since it's my product that I own and manufacture — is to address scamming right there in the product description.

Here's what I say...

> *"Beware fraudulent sellers! They don't have a cheap knockoff version, they do not have a version at all. There is not an item, this is a scam."*

Explaining to people what's going on -- that if they see something that seems too good to be true -- that it probably is, that helps a lot.

SEND AN EMAIL TO AMAZON

The third thing -- the most important thing -- to do is to send an email to Amazon. You don't want to flood them with emails, or you don't pester them with phone calls (it doesn't work) but you do need to reach out.

The email is seller-performance@amazon.com — just send them one email per day. If you've got a lot of fraudulent sellers on your account every day, just pick a time of day and then send them an email.

Here's the format and process that I use.

1. Compose an email to seller-performance@amazon.com
2. Subject line: Possible Fraudulent Sellers
3. In the email body, put the name of fraudulent seller's store, with a link to their storefront
4. Do this for however many fraudulent sellers there are
5. Underneath, say, "We believe the above sellers are engaging in fraudulent selling activity. Please investigate."

Presto. They will sort it.

This is what it looks like:

> *To: seller-performance@amazon.com*
> *Subject: Possible Fraudulent Seller*
> *Body:*
>
> *Seller Name: HairWOW (or whoever it is)*
> *Link to their storefront: (paste here)*
>
> *We believe the above seller is engaging in fraudulent selling activity.*
> *lease investigate. Thanks!*

And then you wait. That's all. If there are multiple fraudulent sellers, you can just list them all in one email.

Bonus tip: Lay the smack down!

Because I believe that everyone should be held accountable for their actions, I also go to that fraudulent seller's store and click on the button that says, 'Ask Seller a Question', and I hit them with my standard shaming paragraph:

> *"Didn't your mother teach you not to cheat people out of their money? Don't you know you're hurting people's businesses? This is not a victimless crime. Shame on you."*

I have no idea how many times that's worked, but it makes me feel much better.

I hope that helps you to navigate this more seedy section of Amazon, and that you won't get discouraged from selling on what has to be one of the best platforms we've ever used — after BigCommerce, of course!

09 The Buy Box: How It Works and Why It's So Important

Eyal Lanxner, CTO, Feedvisor

There are two types of sellers on Amazon:

1. Amazon itself, which sells a vast range of products
2. Third-party retailers, who typically specialize in one or more categories.

Since there is no limit to the number of sellers who can use the Amazon platform, multiple merchants frequently sell the same item. These sellers are known as resellers (as compared to private label selling). When multiple resellers are selling at the same time, suddenly there is competition for which seller will win the Buy Box.

What's changed since 2016?

1. What Happened to Perfect Order Percentage Score? This metric, which used to have a high impact on the Buy Box, has been removed from Seller Central. We explain this further in this guide, and walk you through Shipping Time as the newest, very important factor in winning the Buy Box.
2. Introducing the Buy Box for Books: Amazon will introduce a Buy Box for new books, allowing booksellers to compete with Amazon for the first time.
3. An Increase in Price Wars: This past year has seen an upswing in price wars, indicating that winning the Buy Box has become even more competitive than before.
4. New Research About the Buy Box: Northeastern University's recent study explores the link between algorithmic repricing, higher prices, and winning the Buy Box.

What is Amazon's Buy Box?

The Buy Box refers to the white box on the right side of the Amazon product detail page, where customers can add items for purchase to their cart.

Not all sellers are eligible to win the Buy Box.

Thanks to stiff competition and Amazon's customer-obsessed approach, only businesses with excellent seller metrics stand a chance to win a share of this valuable real estate.

To get a sense of how incredibly important prioritizing the Buy Box is, consider this: 82% of Amazon's sales go through the Buy Box, and the percentage is even higher for mobile purchases.

Understanding the way Amazon's algorithms function will allow you to work toward increasing your performance on relevant variables, ultimately increasing your chances of winning the Buy Box and beating the competition.

The Essential Buy Box Elements

While we refer to the goal of winning the Buy Box, it's perhaps more accurate to say that a seller wins or loses a share of the Buy Box.

Once a merchant has passed Amazon's minimum eligibility requirements, the Buy Box algorithm further breaks down the sellers according to different variables.

Amazon puts the competitors against each other to determine how they hold up on each variable for the same product.

For more popular items with many sellers, multiple merchants may rotate their spot on the Buy Box. If one seller is stronger than the rest, their percentage share of the Buy Box will be higher.

For example, the top-ranking seller of a product could hold the Buy Box for 70% of the day, while the lower-ranking seller could hold it for the remaining 30% of the day.

Amazon's Balancing Act

Ultimately, Amazon tries to balance giving the consumer the best value for their money; this is done by weighing low prices with high seller metrics.

What this means, among other things, is that if you have near-perfect performance metrics, you may be able to price higher and still obtain the Buy Box. Whereas if you have mid-range metrics, you'll probably need to focus on offering the most competitive price.

> **There isn't one magic element, but a whole host of factors that go into deciding who wins.**

You might be thinking:

- Well, doesn't that only work if I'm competing against other third party sellers?
- But what about when the competitor is Amazon itself?
- Hasn't Amazon perfected its customer performance metrics?

Well, it's true that Amazon is hard to beat. But if you have great metrics, as well as very low prices, it is possible. At the very least, you can share the Buy Box with Amazon.

What Makes You Buy Box Eligible?

What are the requirements for competing for the Buy Box? While there's no surefire formula to landing in — or winning — the Buy Box rotation, there are four minimum criteria you must meet if you want to be in the running:

1. Professional Seller Account: Only sellers who have purchased a Professional Seller account (in Europe called a Pro-Merchant account) are eligible. An individual seller (in Europe: Basic account) is not.
2. Buy Box Eligibility: Your status can be checked in Amazon Seller Central.
3. New Items: Your item must be new. Used items aren't eligible for the regular Buy Box, though they can be sold on a separate Buy Used Box.
4. Availability: There needs to be inventory of your listed item. Without stock, the Buy Box will simply rotate to another seller.

Buy Box Alternatives

Winning the Buy Box is not the only way to sell on Amazon. The two other options are through:

- Other Sellers on Amazon
- The Offer Listing Page.

While these aren't as profitable as the Buy Box, they will still give you a degree of visibility.

OTHER SELLERS ON AMAZON

Right under the Buy Box is a listing of up to three select listings. These listings must still meet all the above Buy Box requirements. While not as visible as the Buy Box, these do have a greater chance of conversion than those prices or brands not showing up at all.

OFFER LISTING PAGE

This page lists all the sellers who sell a particular product, regardless of whether they're Buy Box eligible. Offerings are displayed in order of Landed Price (price + shipping). Customers can also see other seller variables including buyer feedback and rebate policies.

The Rising Importance of Buy Box Mobile

More customers than ever are shopping on Amazon via mobile.

Amazon reported that during the 2016 holiday period, 72% of their customers worldwide shopped via mobile, purchasing at extremely high frequencies.

The Amazon app is free for most mobile devices and its look and feel is similar to their main sites.

In mobile, the Buy Box takes on heightened importance. That's because unlike on a desktop or laptop, the mobile site features the Buy Box directly under the product image.

Customers click "Buy now" to place their order, without the Offer Listing page being in their line of sight. Note that there is no "Other Sellers on Amazon" box displayed on the mobile Amazon site. Only the name of the Buy Box winner is displayed. If you care about reaching mobile shoppers, that's another reason to prioritize winning the Buy Box.

4 Key Metrics That Amazon's Buy Box Algorithm Looks For

First and foremost, here's a quick little takeaway for you –– the Buy Box Cheat Sheet of all thematics that matter to get your brand in the box.

While there are many variables that influence your chances of winning the Buy Box and getting favored by Amazon's algorithms, there are four that have the highest Buy Box impact:

1. Using Fulfillment By Amazon
2. Seller-Fulfilled Prime
3. Landed Price
4. Shipping Time

1. FULFILLMENT BY AMAZON (FBA)

> ### The variable that has the greatest impact on the Buy Box is the product's fulfillment method.

Since Amazon considers its fulfillment service to have perfect metrics across variables, using Fulfillment By Amazon (FBA) is the easiest way to increase your chances of winning the Buy Box.

That's not to say that Fulfillment By Merchant (FBM) sellers can never beat FBA sellers; it's just harder, requiring extremely high scores across all variables and a very low price. Even though FBA is often a smart choice, you still need to look at the big picture to evaluate whether it will save or cost you in the end.

2. SELLER-FULFILLED PRIME

Seller-Fulfilled Prime offers top-performing Fulfillment By Merchant (FBM) sellers the opportunity to fulfill their orders while enjoying the benefits of Amazon Prime.

This fulfillment method offers the best of both worlds:

- **You maintain control over your own shipment**, which is especially good for sellers with heavy products, who can use this method to bypass FBA's extra fees.
- **You will also benefit by having a higher chance to win the Buy Box** and getting access to Prime members.

The only potential downside is that not all FBM sellers are eligible for this method. Very strong overall metrics are a must if you want to qualify.

3. LANDED PRICE

The landed price refers to the total price an Amazon product goes for, including shipping.

> **The lower the landed price, the greater the Buy Box share.**

If you have higher performance metrics than your direct competitors, you can also price higher and retain your share of the Buy Box. If, however, your competitors have better metrics, you'll need to price down to maintain the same Buy Box share.

4. SHIPPING TIME

The simplest metric looked at by the Buy Box is the time in which the seller promises to ship the item to the customer.

For certain time-critical products and categories, such as birthday cards and perishable goods, the impact of this metric on the Buy Box will be even higher, since customers often demand swift shipping on such items.

Buy Box Pricing Strategies: Manual vs. Rule-Based vs. Algorithmic

The go-to method of pricing for many sellers has been to lower their prices beyond that of their competitors to increase their chances of securing the Buy Box. However, this does not always translate into higher profits for reasons described below.

There are three methods of repricing used on Amazon:

1. Manual
2. Rule-based
3. Algorithmic

MANUAL REPRICING

Manual repricing involves manually updating your prices for each ASIN. It's an ideal option for sellers of homemade or unique goods but proves inefficient and inaccurate for sellers of competitive items. As your business grows, this method is generally considered unsustainable.

RULE-BASED REPRICING

Rule-based repricing examines the prices of the competition and reprices according to predefined rules. For example, you can set a rule that beats the competitor by a certain amount or stay in the lowest price bracket.

This method is easier than manual repricing, but it also has some major downsides:

- By only looking into competitors' pricing, it is limited in its capabilities.
- Setting up the rules is a time-consuming task, and rules can come into conflict with each other, requiring excessive management.

Finally, rule-based repricers often leave money on the table because sellers who could afford to price higher (due to high seller metrics) and still maintain their share of the Buy Box, don't. And it tends to create price wars, with all sellers constantly lowering their prices, ultimately driving profits down for everyone.

ALGORITHMIC REPRICING

Algorithmic repricing is considered the most sophisticated and revolutionary repricing option. Unlike rule-based repricing, which only focuses on the competitors' prices, algorithmic repricing takes into account all the variables that affect your chances of winning the Buy Box.

A recent Northeastern University study found a direct correlation between algorithmic repricing, higher Buy Box share and increased profitability. By monitoring a wide range of important factors, it ensures that you are striking the right balance between Buy Box share and profit. This data-driven approach has been proven to deliver the highest ROI for merchants, as it requires less effort and yields better results. This repricing method is, however, the most expensive out of all the available options, and is, therefore, best suited for larger sellers who are already turning high profits.

WRAP UP

There is no one trick to beating the Buy Box, but rather a complex web of metrics to be monitored and improved upon. Concentrating on the most important variables, such as becoming an FBA seller, having Prime-eligible products, perfecting your customer service, and understanding the way pricing works, are all key to snagging that coveted Buy Box real estate.

In the end, you're going to have to be algorithmic about your strategy –– the same way Amazon is.

> *"If you're that one lucky seller who gets the 'Buy Box,' you make all the sales," says assistant professor Christo Wilson, lead researcher of the Northeastern University study. "So if you want to be competitive for the top-selling products, you pretty much have no choice: You have to be an algorithmic seller."*

10 How to Master Amazon SEO & Move Your Products to Page 1

Bryan Bowman, AMZ Profit Pros Founder

Looking back on the past two years, I'm still amazed at the river of money Amazon has provided for so many people –– from stay-at-home moms to major household brands.

And while it's not always good news (nothing ever is in business), the opportunity is still very real and I believe will continue to get even better.

However, as more competition has entered the marketplace, it means sellers must bring their best cards to the table if they're going to win.

When ask to write this chapter, I was thrilled.

I wanted to write a comprehensive guide that not only explained how Amazon's search engine works, but the specific methods and tools my team is using today to help our clients optimize their listings and crush it on Amazon.

This type of guide simply didn't exist ... until now.

The beauty and burden of Amazon's search engine -- aka A9 -- is its simplicity. Amazon provides a very simple-to-use interface where sellers can populate all the data relevant to their product. Once you know what to put in these fields, it makes it very easy to implement any changes.

However, because A9 is a maturing algorithm, frequent and unpredictable updates are a common point of frustration for many sellers on Amazon. In turn, I've done my best to include the most up-to-date recommendations and tips based on both Amazon's documentation and our own observations after managing 1000s of Amazon listings.

However, the observations and recommendations I make in this guide are subject to change as A9 evolves. Therefore, I encourage you to revisit this guide frequently and check the comments section often.

How To Get a 320% Increase in Sales in Less Than 10 Minutes

One of my favorite clients in the entire world is Debbie. In one word, she's awesome. She has passion and truly believes in her products and how they can improve people's lives.

Unfortunately, that passion didn't translate into many sales because she wasn't into all that "technical stuff" and she had done a poor job of building a solid listing.

In fact, she had done a very poor job -- like "how have you even sold a unit?" poor job. So, on day one my team decided to focus on three parts of her listing:

1. Images
2. Title
3. Backend search terms.

You'll learn why these are so important in a bit. She made the changes and, within 10 minutes, they were updated and live. Then, we waited.

Before working together, Debbie was selling about five units per day, give or take a unit or two. The next morning, I woke up to four missed text messages.

> **She made two sales before 7 a.m. -- this had never happened. By the end of that day, she had made 16 sales. This has been the new normal ever since.**

While I can't guarantee a 320% increase in sales, I can assure you this chapter will help you bring your absolute best to Amazon so you're ready to compete.

I'll first cover a bit about Amazon, A9 and ranking factors in the algorithm.

Then, I'll dive deep into how to create killer listings optimized for the right search terms that help us to compete with and crush our competition.

The One Thing To Remember for Amazon SEO

If you only get one thing from this chapter, it should be this:

> *Amazon cares about buyers and selling stuff to those buyers.*

That's it.

Yes, that is quite possibly the most obvious statement made by anyone ever. But, if you can remember this anytime you are making changes to your listings, and balance that with your own interests, you'll quickly start making decisions that will help your products sell on Amazon.

What differentiates A9 from Google Search or other top search engines is Amazon is a buying platform. As consumers, we rarely hop on Amazon just for product research. We are usually very close to the point of purchase. Amazon knows this.

In turn, Amazon will continually make changes to test what makes shoppers buy more frequently. Therefore, we need to make changes that will help shoppers convert more frequently.
This includes making our products more visible than our competitor's, so shoppers find us more often. Additionally, we need to make changes that turn browsers to buyers.

- Should you have more images?
- What should you put in the title?
- What price should you sell at?

Just remember, Amazon cares about buyers and selling stuff to those buyers. Help Amazon and you'll help yourself.

Say Hello to A9

I'm going to talk a bit about Amazon's search engine, but only if you promise not to start using "A9" in every other sentence when you're talking to other sellers. As mentioned earlier, it's definitely a maturing algorithm and will continue to become more complex over time.

> **However, for the time being, it operates on what appears to be a very simple keyword search method without much, if any, regard for how closely a product matches the query.**

Let me show you an example below. I've used the customer search term "Dr tobias multivitamin" and you can see there are 3 results:

When I simply add my name "Bryan" to the search, there are no results because Dr. Tobias doesn't have my name anywhere in their product listing -- which is nice to know, I guess.

In a more relevant example, look at the search results for "multivitamin" and the number of results that appear.

Now, look at how the competition gets dramatically reduced when I simply using the variation "multi vitamin":

The competition is cut significantly -- by more than half -- by simply adding a common variation of the search query.

What does that tell you?

AMAZON SEO TIP #1

Make sure you're populating as many relevant terms as possible for your listing if you want to increase your visibility, sales and overall rank in the search results. We'll discuss the how in a bit.

Essentially there are three things you need to optimize for:

- Visibility
- Relevance
- Conversions.

More simply, you want to make sure customers will see, click and buy your product. According to Amazon:

> "Customers must be able to find your products before they can buy your products. Search is the primary way that customers use to locate products on Amazon. Customers search by entering keywords, which are matched against the information (title, description etc.) you provide for a product.
>
> Factors such as degree of text match, price, availability, selection, and sales history help determine where your product appears in a customer's search results. By providing relevant and complete information for your product, you can increase your product's visibility and sales. Below are some general guidelines to improve your product listings."

So, let's have a look at the different pieces of the listing and how we can start optimizing each of them. I'll cover the different ranking factors in the categories:

- Product
- Performance
- Anecdotal.

For anecdotal, there's no supporting Amazon documentation; however, we've seen a strong correlation between Amazon Search Engine Ranking Position (SERP) and these factors.

The recommendations I'm going to make below are just that, recommendations.

I highly encourage you to understand your contract with Amazon and their terms of service. In particular, the documentation on listing optimization.

Product Optimization

TITLE: THE MOST VALUABLE REAL ESTATE ON YOUR LISTING

By far, your product title is the part of your listing that will have the greatest impact (both positive and negative) on product performance in search.

According to Amazon, your title should contain elements such as:

- Brand
- Product Line
- Material or Key Feature
- Product Type
- Color
- Size
- Packaging/Quantity

The secret to an effective title is how you order these elements along with one other major ranking factor: additional target keywords.

In our experience, keyword order and keyword choice can dramatically influence product sales and rank.

First let's discuss order, then we'll address our favorite way to determine the best keyword choices for a particular product. Amazon has 3 different advertising slots –– and in each, the number of characters in the title is different.

- Title in organic results typically have between 115-144 characters depending on the product/category.
- Titles in right rail ads have around 30-33 characters and mobile titles have between 55-63 characters.

So what does that tell us?

We must place the absolute most relevant keywords first. This has both practical and algorithmic implications.

From a practical standpoint, we want to make sure every customer, regardless of search result location, knows exactly what we're selling.

From a practical standpoint, we want to make sure every customer, regardless of search result location, knows exactly what we're selling. Anecdotally, the algorithm correlates higher relevance with keywords that appear earlier in the title.

Therefore, **we recommend making a list of your most important keywords and strategically placing them before each character breakpoint in the title.**

One very common question with clients is if they should use the brand name in the title or not. This particular company has chosen to use VITA ONE at the beginning of the title. Additionally, Amazon's style guide recommends leading with the brand name. Frankly, this is something you should test with your own product to see what converts best.

We generally always lead with the brand name to establish our clients' brands as legitimate companies and not generic "multivitamins."

One thing to note, don't keyword stuff your titles. This was a common strategy a few years back. Both shoppers and Amazon are wise to this and it's no longer effective and may results in an adverse impact to sales. The backend search terms, however, are a great place to keyword stuff and we'll cover that shortly.

Optimizing Amazon Product Titles: Action Steps

Whether you have an existing listing or a brand new one, chances are you can always make some tweaks to help optimize for more visibility and sales. The challenge with a brand new listing is you don't have any product data to lean on, so it's important to see what's currently working for your competitors and replicate that.

Fortunately, there are tools that help us determine what's working. My two favorite tools are Helium 10 – Magnet and Keyword Inspector.

By looking at competitor listings and using these tools, we can determine the best words and placement to start with. From there, we can use Amazon PPC to gather data on which terms help our listing convert and optimize for those keywords. We call it the "optimization cycle" (sounds fancy right?).

The steps are actually pretty straightforward.

1. Use Magnet to research the most popular two or three keywords for your product.
2. Additionally, use Keyword Inspector to do an 'Extensive Reverse ASIN' search on your top competitor.
3. Try to pick a competitor in the top three spots with the most reviews. This is generally an indication they've been selling longer which will provide more data.
4. Once you have these 3-4 sets of data, combine them and remove any search terms that are irrelevant to your product.
5. Then, use a word and two-word phrase frequency counter and start writing out your title based on this frequency.

A great Amazon SEO tool that can help with this is The Helium 10 Scribbles Tool. You'll want to make sure the title reads naturally, yet contains all of the essential elements of the product along with target keywords. Again, look at your top competitors for guidance.

Make use of special characters, like the ones below, to add some style and naturally break up phrases:

|

,

&

–

Next, let's discuss the bullets and how we can further entice shoppers to buy.

BULLETS: ANOTHER CHANCE TO INCREASE CONVERSIONS, RELEVANCE AND RANK

While the bullet points don't directly impact your rank in the search results, they are an opportunity to influence two very important factors in the SERP:

- conversion rate
- product relevance.

The listing bullets are an opportunity to present the features and benefits of your product. Most sellers will tell you they know this, yet I'm surprised how often people get their product features and their product benefits mixed up.

For example, **leather seats are a feature and the feeling of luxury and arriving refreshed are benefits.**

Also, just like the title, words used in the bullets will be indexed by the algorithm and used to help identify your product when customers use the search bar. However, in our experience, terms in the bullets don't carry the same weight as those in the title.

OPTIMIZING PRODUCT BULLETS: ACTION STEPS

Essentially, whatever keywords weren't used in the title, from the master list you compiled earlier, should be worked into the bullets.

> **Again, Helium 10 – Scribbles is an awesome tool for building out your listing as it simultaneously eliminates words from your master list as you populate your listing details.**

This is also a good time to point out products your listing may be compatible with. For example, if you're selling a phone case you may point out several brands and models it's compatible with.

Hint: In most cases, these terms will get indexed so your listing can appear for searches like "Samsung phone case" or "Galaxy S7 phone case."

Also, if you have a product warranty, most sellers will typically include these details in the last bullet. In general, we highly recommend testing the copy and order of the bullet points.

On occasion, we've seen different combinations result in higher conversions.

PRODUCT DESCRIPTION: TELL A STORy

Much like the bullet points, the product description doesn't directly impact rank. However, it is indexed and will impact visibility. Additionally, well-written copy with a strong call to action can certainly have an effect on conversions.

> **This is a great time to tell a bit about your brand and product, while throwing in some valuable keywords you want indexed.**

Also, make sure to include a strong call to action at the end. Make it direct and to the point (i.e. Buy Now, Order Today, etc.).

OPTIMIZING PRODUCT DESCRIPTION: ACTION STEPS

Again, this is a great opportunity to keep using the Helium 10 – Scribbles Tool and include as many keywords as you can while still writing engaging copy.

Another tip is to make use of simple HTML. My favorite tool for converting text to HTML is Word to Clean HTML.

It's free and very easy-to-use. Simply paste your formatted text and click convert. You can then paste the HTML into your product detail page.

BACKEND SEARCH TERMS: KEYWORD STUFF LIKE IT'S 2014...I'M KIDDING, SORT OF

Way back in the early days of Amazon FBA, around 12-18 months ago, people would create the ugly keyword-stuffed titles, bullets and descriptions.
Like really ugly:

Thankfully, the market and the algorithm will penalize you for this type of behavior. However, there is a place you can stuff all of the remaining keywords from your master list:

the backend search terms!

These terms are not visible to customers, yet get indexed just like the terms in your bullets and description — similar to the now-outdated meta keywords HTML tag.

This is a great place to type any terms that will complete and long tail searches as well.

For example, if you sell a sleeping bag and couldn't stylishly insert the terms "...for camping that fits 2 big boned people," the backend search terms are perfect for that.

HOW TO USE BACKEND SEARCH TERMS

Backend Search Terms are also a great place to drop some Spanish terms, misspellings and words commonly used in your niche.

For example, if I sold dog accessories, I may include the top 50 or 100 dog breeds since most owners will search "dog collar for Labrador."

As for misspellings, Amazon says they account for them but our experience shows otherwise, so we include them.

BACKEND SEARCH TERMS: ACTION

Just like before, keep using your Helium 10 – Scribbles Tool to knock out the remaining terms you didn't capture in the title, bullets and description.

THERE'S NO NEED FOR COMMAS

Just separate the terms with a space. Another thing to note is you don't need to duplicate keywords in your listing. Once a term is typed in the title, bullets, description or backend search terms, you don't need to repeat it anywhere else.

Performance Optimization

SALES ARE KING

After all the testing we've done, nothing moves the search rank needle like sales. In particular, your sales velocity relative to your competition.

> **A spike in sales that your competition didn't see will dramatically impact your ranking position.**

As you can imagine, this is very can be tough to accomplish when you first list and appear somewhere on page 20 -- especially when only 30% of customers ever make it to page 2!

Your first option for generating sales is by driving both internal and external traffic to your Amazon listing. This is part of the full management service we offer our clients.

You drive internal traffic via Amazon PPC and external traffic via outside ads like Facebook, Google AdWords, etc.

Commonly, AMZ Profit Pro clients will use one of the following strategies for their external traffic:

- Ad to Amazon Listing
- Ad to Pre-Sell Page to Amazon Listing
- Ad to Squeeze Page to Opt-In for Single Use Discount Code delivered by email
- Ad to Product Sales Funnel

Second, you can use a launch service. Launch services are meant to create a natural spike in sales that moves the product up the ranks.

Ultimately, whether this rank "sticks" will depend on the organic demand for the product once it becomes visible on page 1 or 2. There is some controversy surrounding these services and whether they violate Amazon terms of service.

Instead, I recommend Viral Launch.

They have a proprietary system that can help move products up the SERP without violating Amazon TOS and they happen to have great customer service.

PRODUCT REVIEWS ARE QUEEN

If sales are King then reviews are Queen.

Amazon knows customers rely on reviews to make informed decisions about their purchases.

That is why Amazon has been cracking down so hard on fake review services where people are getting paid to write fake positive reviews — and why improving Amazon reviews is top-of-mind for many sellers. Reviews serve as social proof and let buyers know it's safe to spend their money on your product. Plus, who wants to "be the first to leave a review for this product?"

Additionally, reviews factor heavily into product rank in the search results.

I can recall a product one of our clients launched that started selling really well from day one with no reviews. However, it could never break past the page 5 mark. Once the first two reviews came in, the product jumped to page 2. Sales continued to come in and once the product received it's 10th review, it hit page 1 almost the same day.

The moral of the story is, do what you can to get honest and unbiased reviews as soon as possible.

The Definitive Guide To Selling On Amazon

The first thing to get in place is an email feedback sequence that communicates with buyers through the buyer-seller messaging service in seller central.

Two of our favorite tools are:

- Feedback Genius
- Sales Backer.

With these services, you can write custom email sequences to your buyers that help develop a customer relationship and ask for honest feedback and reviews. If you'd like to launch a discounted product campaign in order to generate sales and reviews, I highly recommend working with Snagshout (same company as Feedback Genius).

I've had the opportunity to speak with the owner of this service and was very impressed by his commitment to making sure their services are always operating within Amazon's terms of service.

Anecdotal Optimization

In this section, I've lumped a few ranking factor observations we've made that aren't directly documented by Amazon but seem to have an impact on the SERP.

1. **FBA**: Items that are Fulfilled by Amazon seem to rank higher than items Fulfilled by Merchant, all else being equal.
2. **Brand Name**: It appears a brand name which also happens to contain the main keywords may help increase organic rank in search.
3. **Seller Name:** Same as brand name, it appears seller name may help increase organic rank if it contains the main keywords for the product.
4. **Other Fields** in the Edit Product Page: Make sure to fill out all applicable fields in the edit product page as some of these have been shown to influence rank position and filtering in search.
5. **Photos:** Not only do quality photos that zoom influence conversions which certainly impacts rank in search, it appears that more photos is positively correlated with rank in the search results.

A FINAL WORD

**If you've made it this far, you're well ahead
of most sellers I've ever met.**

You now know that Amazon's search engine algorithm has a name and you have a solid understanding of how it works.

You also know enough to be dangerous when it comes to the different components of a product detail page and the effect it can have on your rank in the search results, with no SEO service required. Best of all, you have practical action steps you can put into place today.

Finally, I invite you to check out AMZ Profit Pros for more information and video tutorials that will walk you step-by-step through the process outlined in this guide, including how to use all of the Helium 10 tools.

Until next time, keep crushing it in your businesses and reach out if you have any questions, bryan@amzprofitpros.com.

11 How to Successfully Market Products on Amazon & Think like a Buyer

Kevin Rizer, Private Label Podcast Founder

One of the truly remarkable things about Amazon as a platform is that they do so much of the heavy lifting.

What with being the world's largest e-commerce storefront, Amazon brings droves of traffic to your listing. What's more, that traffic is a pool of buyers, ready to purchase, unlike anything else the world has ever seen.

While eyeballs on Google often equate to browsers and researchers, Amazon attracts buyers.

> **A good conversion rate on an Amazon product detail page is widely considered 15%. That's a huge number, often 3-5x that of other ecommerce sites.**

This is because Amazon product page traffic is already in the purchasing mindset. Of course, to make the most of the traffic Amazon drives to your product page, you must make sure that your listing is properly optimized — for search and Amazon marketing best practices. Here are the most critical elements of maximizing conversions on your Amazon listing.

Buyers Judge Products by the Title of a Listing

One of the two most essential elements of an Amazon product detail page is its title. A title tells people what your product is about.

While Amazon wants your title to be short, descriptive and to the point, they do allow for between 150-250 characters. So, there is plenty of room to throw in some keywords to help your product rank for terms buyers often use when searching for your type of product.

Here are the elements to include in your title:
- Brand name
- Name of the product itself
- Any distinguishing features such as color, size or use

For example, if you sell a blue baby pacifier, your title might look something like this:

> *Deluxe Silicone Baby Pacifier - BPA Free - Comfortable for Baby - Easy for Parents - Set of 2 Pacifiers by Deluxe Baby Gear - Blue*

Your goal for the title on Amazon should be two-fold:

1. to inject a few of the best possible keywords for your product
2. to educate customers more about your product, before even coming to your product page.

It is important not to cram your title so full of keywords that it doesn't make sense. It should be easily readable, and shoppers should be able to tell what your product is immediately.

You can use tools such as Merchant Words, Google Keyword Planner and Simple Keyword Inspector to find relevant keywords for your product type and to estimate search volume.

You can also begin typing in a keyword in Amazon's search bar, and look at the results that populate below as 'recommended' search terms.

This is called Amazon's A9 algorithm, and it is based on the most popular related terms.

Images are Emotional Recognition Tools

Another critical area of importance on an Amazon product details page are images. Images, perhaps more than anything else, can cause a shopper to either click on your listing or to keep scrolling.

> **For this reason, you should spend the time and effort to use high quality images for your product.**

To capture buyer interest and land them on your product page (where there is a 15% conversion rate!), spend the time and effort to use high-quality images for your product. If you have an independent online store, you can use images that work well there. But, Amazon does have a few of its own rules.

AMAZON PRODUCT IMAGE RULES

Amazon requires that the main image for your product include only the product that you are selling, on a white background.

This allows for the search results on Amazon to appear clear, uncluttered and uniform. Amazon tests everything, and they determined in the early days of their existence that visitors to their site bought more — much more –– when products were displayed against a plain white background.

Main images should not include accessories that are not included in the purchase, models or action shots of the image, nor text or badges such as 'Organic' or 'Made in the USA'.

Once a shopper is on your product page, images are even more critical, and can often be a determining factor as to whether someone purchases your product or not.

> **Depending on your product type and category, Amazon will allow you between 5-9 images for your listing.**

Make an effort to use all of the product images offered, and don't use inferior images just to fill up all allowed spaces. While your main image is required to be against a plain, white background, Amazon allows for other image types on secondary images.

These could include:

- Your product from different angles (side, top, close up)
- The back of a product label

- Images of your product in-action
- Images that list your products features or compare it against other products
- Informational images with text/charts, etc.
- Images that show your product's size as compared to a human holding it

Amazon requires that images be a minimum of 1,000 pixels x 1,000 pixels to take advantage of its zoom feature, which allows buyers to scroll over an image to enlarge it. This is a popular feature with Amazon buyers, so take advantage of it.

> **If you can, use images that are 2,000 pixels x 2,000 pixels, for added granularity.**

My favorite resource for high quality, affordable images is AMZDream.com Once your listing is live, you should test your image placement to see which images elicit the highest conversion rate for your product.

To do this, track your total sessions, number of sales, conversion rate (unit session percentage) and total revenue over the course of a week, then change the order of your images, and measure the same data over the next week. You may find that a certain image order elicits a much higher conversion rate than another.

If They Can't Read It, They Won't Come

For buyers unconvinced by your title and images, your bullet points are your next opportunity to seal the deal. Amazon's bullet points are relatively straightforward. You have five spaces for bullet points, but that does not mean you are limited to five words or even five sentences.

To maximize the use of your bullets, use a short paragraph of two to four sentences and focus on the features and benefits of your product. Address any common questions or objections that might cause someone not to buy.

Remember to update these often!

> **If you get complaints in your reviews that come simply from a misinterpretation of the product, update your bullets (and maybe even your title) to account for that.**

Use the first three bullet points to drive home your product's most important features. Here is an example:

- **LUXURIOUS DOWN FABRIC IS SOFT & ELEGANT** Our premium down comforter hugs you in incredibly silky soft comfort. While other comforters can be scratchy and leave you tossing the covers off, you'll want to snuggle up all night with ours.
- **ADVANCED TEMPERATURE CONTROL KEEPS YOU COMFORTABLE** One of the most annoying things about most down comforters is that they can get too hot. Our patent-pending material regulates your temperature, ensuring you stay at the optimal temperature all night, every night.
- **UNIQUE DESIGN KEEPS DOWN MATERIAL FROM SHIFTING** Using chambers woven together to prevent shifting, our premium down fill remains where it is supposed to be. You'll never have to worry about waking up clinging to an empty comforter again.

Use the fourth and fifth bullets to answer common questions, or overcome other objections common with your product:

- **FITS ALL QUEEN MATTRESSES** Our down comforter has been designed to fit all queen mattresses. Don't risk a bad fit with an inexpensive comforter. Insist on the best.
- **100% 90 DAY MONEY BACK GUARANTEE** If you are not satisfied for any reason, simply return your comforter for a full refund, no questions asked. You have nothing to lose.

Using all caps for the beginning of your bullets can help you to emphasize key points.

Note that Amazon does not allow a 'Seller Warranty' but does allow for a 'Manufacturer's Warranty' to be included in a listing.

Amazon offers all buyers protection under its A-Z Guarantee program, which all sellers are required to abide by and honor.

Engagement Isn't Just a 10-Letter Word (Or Is It?)

The product description area is perhaps your last chance to turn a shopper into a buyer on your Amazon listing. Despite its importance on independent webstores, the product description is often overlooked by Amazon shoppers. This might be because of it's location on the page:

Buried toward the bottom and without any pomp and circumstance to draw attention.

Amazon allows for basic HTML to be used in the product description, which includes:

- Bold
- Italics
- Quotes
- Line breaks
- Page breaks.

You should use basic HTML markup, if possible, to highlight certain words or phrases, and to make your description easier to read, as opposed to a paragraph all lumped together.

Amazon no longer allows other forms of HTML in the product description or any other areas of an Amazon listing.

ENHANCED BRAND CONTENT

Enhanced Brand Content, previously reserved only for products sold by Amazon, and those sellers in the Vendor program, is now available for most sellers through Seller Central. This exciting new program allows sellers to greatly enhance the Product Description section of their listing with additional photos, copy and even comparison charts.

As of the date of this publishing (Fall 2017), Enhanced Brand Content detail pages are available at no additional cost to sellers.

I highly recommend taking advantage of them.

First Impressions Matter Most

Reviews impact an Amazon product listing in three ways and should be one of your top marketing considerations.

AVERAGE STAR RATING

First, reviews impact product listing placement through the average star rating that appears alongside the product in search results and at the top of the product detail page.

> **A product with an average star rating of 4 or 4.5 stars will typically outperform a similar product with only 3 or 3.5 stars.**

In 2015, Amazon transitioned to a weighted system for measuring a product's average star rating. Things like the below now affect the weighting of each review. This means that the average is not simply a straight mathematical average:

- Whether a product is bought at a discount
- How long ago the review was left
- How helpful other Amazon shoppers say a review is to them

Tip: You can make the most of your average star rating by focusing on courting organic reviews from customers who pay full price for your product.

MOST POPULAR REVIEWS SECTION

The Most Popular Reviews section, which is located toward the middle of the page on the left-hand side, is the area where reviews for the product that have been voted 'Yes" as helpful most often.

> **Sellers cannot dictate which reviews show up in this section.**

Customer votes, whether they have purchased the item or not, can affect which reviews show up here. Typically, the more 4 and 5-star reviews that appear in this section, the higher the conversion rate and sales will be, while the more 1 to 3-star reviews that show up, the lower the conversion rate and sales will be.

The Mountain is proof that people don't have to buy your item for reviews to boost your ranking. In 2008, a college student left a satirical review on the brand's Three Wolf Moon T-shirt. Since then, 40,000 people have said the review was helpful. The Mountain is a now a multi-million dollar brand.

MOST RECENT CUSTOMER REVIEWS

The final place that reviews impact a listing are in the 'Most Recent Customer Reviews' section, which is located towards the middle of the page to the right. This section includes the ten most recent reviews, and cannot be impacted by votes of any kind.

> **The only way for a review to move out of the most recent section is for more reviews to be left for that product, replacing it.**

To maximize your chances for successful selling on Amazon, pay close attention to your reviews. Sell a quality product, treat your customers well, take care of issues promptly when they arise and always go above and beyond.

You can comment on reviews as the seller, and many buyers appreciate a seller that is proactive about addressing issues and providing an exceptional customer experience.

If They Ask, You Should Answer

Perhaps the most underutilized marketing opportunity of an Amazon product listing is the Questions & Answers section.

Questions are submitted by customers, whether they have purchased the product or not. A unique feature is that the answers to these questions can be submitted by both other customers (again, whether they have purchased the product or not) or by the seller.

Many sellers assume that they must simply sit back and wait until customers start asking questions for this section to be utilized. Instead, consider seeding the section by asking a colleague or friend to put a question that is common for your product, so that you can answer it.

Once questions are asked, make sure that the answers displayed to those questions are accurate. If multiple answers are provided by either customers or sellers, Amazon displays the answer that has the most votes.
Votes are submitted by either clicking on the "up" or "down" arrow next to the answer. Because anyone can submit an answer, you will want to keep an eye on this section and ensure that the answer displayed for a question is correct.

Easy Search Terms, Easy Find

In addition to pulling from a title and bullets, Amazon determines which keywords are relevant for your listing from the Search Terms section, which is located in the back end of seller central.

This section is not visible to the public.

In 2017, Amazon began truncating the back-end search terms to the first 250 characters.

That is to say that only these characters are "indexed", and show up in search results.

Because of this, it is now extremely important to make sure your first 250 characters in the Search Terms field are the most relevant to your product listing.

Here are a few guidelines for search terms in Amazon:

- You do not need a comma between words, but you do need a space.
- Include both singular and plural versions of important words, for example 'dog' is not the same as 'dogs.'
- Do not repeat words, or make sentences out of your keywords. For example, once you use the word 'dog,' there is no need to repeat that word anywhere else in the search terms section.

You'll know you are on the right track if you end up with a search terms section that is not cohesive, meaning there are no complete sentences; it should seem like a jumbled up mess of related words. Good job!

Here's an example:

> *dog dogs puppy puppies premium toy toys bone rawhide bones rawhides best natural organic USA made in big chew chews*

A Final Word

We've covered a lot of ground, and laid the groundwork for a great product listing — and marketing plan — on Amazon! It's important, however, to note that a well-performing listing is part science and part art.

Testing is to make sure you are maximizing the opportunity. When testing, make small changes and give adequate time to measure the impact of those changes so that you know whether to keep them or to revert to the previous version of your listing.

If possible, test only one element of your listing at a time. If you test multiple items at once, you will not know which change impacted your listing, however positive or negative the impact.

There are a lot of critical elements to a product's success or failure on the world's largest ecommerce platform. Your listing is certainly a major one, and following these simple steps, you are well on your way to an optimized and high-converting listing.

12 The Secret Amazon Pricing Strategy to Crush the Competition

Kai Klement, KAVAJ Co-Founder, Multi-Million Dollars Amazon Seller

Wrong pricing, fake reviews or just bad customer service can kill your Amazon adventure faster than you think.

To many, this makes Amazon complicated, but...

> **Your strategy on Amazon must be dead simple,
> and lead with the customer in mind.**

Your goal is to generate as many sales as possible, get authentic product reviews and provide the best customer service to your Amazon customers.

In this chapter, I will detail the exact strategies we used to build our private label brand KAVAJ from scratch in 2011.

Further, I'll give you insight into our approach to pricing on Amazon. We are selling our products solely as a marketplace seller via Amazon (Europe, USA, Japan) and have sold more than 500,000 KAVAJ products, making more than $19 million in revenue.

Before we begin, always remember your ultimate goal:

You want your products to be within the top three spots on the first page of the search results for your most relevant keywords.

Further, **you want to build a long-term brand on Amazon which will result in Amazon** promoting your products throughout your product detail page.

In the KAVAJ example below you can see the effect of building a brand on Amazon.

In the "Customers who bought this item also bought" section, Amazon will automatically promote all your other products.
Further, you want to build a long-term brand on Amazon which will result in Amazon promoting your products throughout your product detail page.

In the KAVAJ example below you can see the effect of building a brand on Amazon. In the "Customers who bought this item also bought" section, Amazon will automatically promote all your other products.

Sales, Sales, Sales

OPTIMIZE YOUR PRODUCT DETAIL PAGE

The basics just aren't very good.

Before you even start thinking about generating traffic or putting any marketing budget to work, you have to do the basics. On Amazon, this means you have to optimize your Amazon product detail page for Amazon's organic search results.

The vast majority of sales on Amazon happen through search and more than 70% of it on page one of Amazon search results.

It's best to spend time optimizing your products for Amazon's search. Bryan Bowman details every aspect on this topic in his part "A Seller's Guide to Amazon SEO." Make sure to read that first.

Set Your Prices For Page 1 on Amazon & Know All Your Costs

If you get your pricing wrong, you will either lose money or won't sell anything.

Setting the right price on Amazon doesn't have to be that hard for private label products where you don't have any competition on your Amazon product page.

In general, there are two variables you need to consider for every single product you sell on Amazon.

1. You want to be profitable (Find your lowest price)
2. You want to maximize profits (Find your highest price possible)

First, you need to consider all of your costs, and what your prices would be for you to be profitable on Amazon with those costs included. You need to calculate your floor price.

Second, your price must be competitive related to your most important search terms to get your product on page one of Amazon search results. No one will find and order your overpriced product on page 23.

More than 70% of sales on Amazon happen on page one of organic search.

CALCULATE YOUR FLOOR PRICE

To operate in the green, you need to know all your costs, take all of them into account, and then determine your price floor. You can find below the list of costs which you have to take into your equation.

Product Acquisition Cost
- Shipping
- Customs
- Payment wiring
- Amazon Commission
- Amazon FBA Fees

- Customer Return Fees
    - On all returns, Amazon keeps 20% of the original commission as a return fee
- Your own returns-related fees
    - return shipping fees
    - disposal fees
    - product write-offs fees
- Variable overhead allocation costs

There are also category-specific costs which you need to consider. For example, if you sell clothing, Amazon will charge you FBA fees related to customer return shipping costs.

FIND YOUR UPPER PRICE FLOOR

Forget about overpricing your product!
Amazon will tell you your upper price floor.

Always remember, your ultimate goal is to have your products ranked on page 1 of Amazon search results. This is where the magic happens, and you can really sell volume.

However, it is one thing to get your products to page one with deep marketing pockets (e.g. deep launch discounts, giveaways or a big Amazon Sponsored Products budget), but y**ou want your product to stay on page one and generate sustainable, profitable organic sales.**

To get your products to stick on page one, you must consider the competition around you.

This is easy to evaluate. Just search your top three keywords for your product and review the pricing of the search results on page one.

Now, answer this question: **are your prices within a reasonable range of the prices you find there?**

From our experience, you can be 20% more expensive
than the highest price on page one of search results.

For example, the highest price you can find on page one is $40. Your upper price floor thus should be $48. If your price is higher, you will most likely never make it to the top of Amazon search results.

KEEP YOUR PRICES STABLE, WITH EXCEPTIONS

To build customer trust and a sustainable long-term brand on Amazon, keep your prices stable.There are, of course, exceptions.

1. The number one reason for price deviations is to increase your sales rank, which results in more organic sales later.
2. The second reason for price cuts is cross-selling your products, which in the end also results in better sales rank for all products included in the cross-selling promotion.

Usually, this means cutting your prices close to break-even or below profitability. This is most often done during new product launches.

My company deviates from our standard prices mainly in the following contexts:

*   **New Product Launches**
    - We offer 15% launch discount for all customers
    - We offer up to 50% price cuts for repeat customers on our email list
*   **Cross Selling**
    - We offer up to 40% discount for bundles sales. e.g. If a customer buys an iPad case,   he will get a 40% discount for an Apple pencil case
*   **Black Friday or Other Holidays**
*   **Stock Clearance**
    - In case you have overstock, this can help get rid of your overstock. It can also revive a dead product.

Finally, before you even think about cutting prices below profitability, always keep in mind that you will only have fun (i.e. be successful) selling on Amazon once you can generate organic sales with a decent profit margin.

Drive Traffic to your Amazon Products

Without traffic, there are no sales. Just listing your product on Amazon and hoping for traffic and sales is not enough to be successful. Today, you need not only the organic traffic on Amazon, but you need to drive traffic from external sources to your Amazon product page.

Here's a quick story to really drive this home.

Paris, here we come...

Not long after leaving Amazon to start my own company, my team and I had a brilliant marketing idea. We were so convinced that it would work that we boarded a plane from Germany to France.

Before we left, we printed off thousands of flyers and planned on handing them out in front of the Apple store in Paris. We knew that tons of people would be standing in front of the store waiting to get their new device, and we knew that we would have a captive audience. We gave away every single flyer that we brought.

People genuinely seemed interested in our product.

- They liked the design
- They liked meeting us as the creators
- We had several promising conversations that we believed would turn into sales.

When we got home to Germany, we were eager to check our dashboard for sales. We logged in and were totally shocked. We had sold just one case.

JUST ONE.

We immediately knew we had to change our strategy to drive traffic to our products. Here are our the 3 key strategies we are using today to drive most of our traffic to our Amazon product pages.

1. BUILD AN EMAIL LIST

An email list is a great way to boost your sales at product launch. We use our list to send our customers directly to our new product pages on Amazon. We also give them a discount code for the purchase of the products and often see a good jump start on sales from that.

As a seller on Amazon, you might be wondering how you can build a list since you don't get the real email addresses from customers and also are not allowed to write them for marketing reasons.

Begin with these three, easy-to-implement ways to start building your own list:

1. **Add a signup field on your website**, like a newsletter sign up, an ebook download, or the like.
2. **Communicate your newsletter sign-up option** on your social media channels and on your packaging. Many brands now use Instagram Story to reveal discounts and deals –– let people know there that if they sign up for your newsletter, you will be sending out discounts.
3. **After your sale at Amazon, you can send one email to your customer.** Point them to your newsletter sign up page in this email.

Our current tool of choice is ConvertKit, which has a very easy-to-use interface and allows us to easily tag our customers and build individual newsletter campaigns.

PLACE TARGETED FACEBOOK ADS

In 2014 we shifted a big part of our external ads budget from Google to Facebook. Today, like so many other brands, Facebook Ads are our most important external paid traffic source.

On Facebook, you have multiple advertising options, and you don't need an existing fan base for that.

> **The great thing about Facebook Ads is that you can define your target audience and create a post which will show up directly in a user's Facebook feed.**

For example, for our new iPhone 6 cases, we created a target audience for women between 30 and 35 with kids younger than 3 years AND an interest in photography. We generated awesome results from these ads.
We only had one issue with our Facebook Ads: we could not tell if the ads were profitable. We spent one-and-a-half years developing analytics with quantified markets. Today, it is impossible for us to imagine doing business without analytics –– and now you have the opportunity to use it as well! Working with this Amazon conversion tracking tool catapulted our Facebook marketing performance into entirely new dimensions.

The bottom line is that with analytics, you finally know whether:

- Your Facebook advertising is worthwhile
- You are really addressing the target groups that buy your products on Amazon
- Your advertising is actually generating revenue

Use Amazon Sponsored Product Placements

Amazon Sponsored Products is by far the fastest way to get your product on the first page of Amazon search results.

> **Amazon Sponsored Products work similar to Google AdWords, where you bid on search terms.**

If a person is searching on Amazon for your product, you can buy an ad relative to those search terms, and your offer will appear next to the best results.

The great thing about Amazon Sponsored Products is that it is very easy to setup. You can do it in a matter of minutes.

We did realize pretty early in the process, though, that even in a simple interface, you have to manage your account carefully and regularly to avoid an exploding marketing budget.

There are two main reasons for this.

1. **First, Amazon is continually improving the algorithm**, meaning your successful campaign today will lose money tomorrow.
2. **Second, the competition on your ads is getting tougher as more sellers enter the marketplace.** Amazon has also opened the sponsored products program to Amazon Retail clients.

I recommend either having someone in-house watching your campaigns very closely or working with MarketPlaceClicks, who is managing our account for us.

POINT ALL PRODUCT LINKS ON YOUR WEBSITE AND SOCIAL MEDIA CHANNELS TO AMAZON.

You might ask: "Why should I send my customers over to Amazon if I already have my own website?" The number one reason is that your ultimate goal is to be on the first page of the search results and, if possible, in the top three listing. This is where the big money is made, not by a single sale on your site.

Apart from our website, we point every link on Facebook, Twitter, YouTube, Instagram, our blog posts and our email newsletter to one specific Amazon product page.

Note: You can build high search engine ranking for your own online store through content marketing and influencer outreach work to gain backlinks from relevant, high-quality sites.

GET YOUR PRODUCTS IN THE HANDS OF BLOGGERS AND YOUTUBERS.

YouTube is the second biggest search engine in the world. It's really good to have a ton of reviews about your products on there so that you show up first in search no matter where they search for you.

Remember, Google owns YouTube.

Choose the YouTubers and bloggers who fit best with your product and brand, and offer them free review samples. Here are few tips for outreach:

- Be sure to word your outreach genuinely, and help solve a problem for their audience.
- Know that they receive tons of these emails regularly.
- Keep a running list of who you are reaching out to and who responds.
- Use this to build yourself an influencer list.

If you give your products away for review, only give them your top selling product. Put all your eggs in one basket. Remember, you want to have this product in the top three of the first page of search results, so you have to ensure that all the traffic is going to that one product.

MAXIMIZE YOUR PRODUCT PACKAGING.

Every case we ship includes a small booklet and two business card sized inserts with 10% discount codes for customers to give their friends or use on their next Amazon order of a KAVAJ product.

> **Customers are telling their friends about us and they're buying more cases for themselves.**

We also use our best customer testimonials to build trust. We put our best quote on the outside packaging and, for our most important products, we include a customer case study inside a small booklet.

CREATE EFFECTIVE GOOGLE AD CAMPAIGNS.

We spent a lot of money on Google in our early days. However, Facebook Ads and Amazon Sponsored Products totally changed the game.

Today, you should use Google AdWords as follows:

- **Focus on brand name:** Focus your efforts on your brand name and the most specific keywords in the long tail. We get most of the traffic from Google from people searching for our brand "KAVAJ."
- **Focus on long-tail keywords:** In the long tail, we only create very specific campaigns for our products, which must include the device name, the material, and the color. For example, those words that are keywords to our product, phrases like "iPad Air 2 case leather black."

Get Real Product Reviews

Without product reviews, you won't sell anything on Amazon. The amount and the quality of reviews are the most important aspects of your reviews to increase your conversion rate.

Unfortunately, only 1 out of 100 customers writes a review.

Here are a few ways to increase your number of authentic product reviews.

*WARNING: Before getting into the details, this subject requires a quick warning, as Amazon is currently cracking down on sellers buying fake reviews. **Never mess with Amazon.** Avoid review clubs and excessive giveaways, which do not comply with Amazon's Terms of Services (ToS).*

Don't give away a free product in exchange for an Amazon review. Your goal should be to build trust with your customers and a long-term brand on Amazon.

Even if the customer is leaving a disclaimer that he got the product for free, it will hurt your product and there is a high chance that Amazon will either delete all those reviews or even suspend your seller account.

This is what you should do instead.

EMAIL YOUR CUSTOMERS AFTER PURCHASE AND ASK FOR REVIEWS.

You can use tools like Feedback Genius to automate this process.

1. Send the email a few days after the purchase.
2. Ask in a neutral way and don't force them to leave a positive review.
3. Provide a direct link to the review page, as a lot of your customers have probably never written a review before.

You can also use this opportunity to make sure the product was delivered correctly and give the customer a chance to tell you about their experience (good or bad) so you can make the most of the interaction and build lifetime brand loyalty.

USE "WRONG" POSITIVE SELLER FEEDBACK TO GET PRODUCT REVIEWS.

People often confuse seller feedback with product reviews. Unfortunately, the often really good product feedback is not very visible for other customers.

Review your seller feedback regularly for people who actually provide positive product feedback and ask them via email to also write a product review.

COMMENT ON REVIEWS.

Everything on the Amazon product page is public.

In particular, the reviews and comments sections will be read by almost all future customers. This is your chance to stand out.

Be sure to comment on any negative product reviews or on reviews where a customer has a question. This is your opportunity to build trust and increase your conversion.

Further, many customers who initially gave your product a negative review might even change it for a positive one because they are grateful that you cared about their issue.

ASK CUSTOMERS WHO EMAIL YOU FOR FEEDBACK.

The easiest way to get product reviews on Amazon is by simply asking customers who tell you how much they love your product.

Whenever you receive an email, a customer service call or positive feedback on your social media channels, just ask them politely if they are willing to share their experience with other customers on Amazon.

Provide Outstanding Customer Service

You can't do anything wrong if your Amazon customer benefits. Amazon itself is the most customer-centric company in the world.

They expect the same standard from you as a seller. Your best marketing tool on Amazon today will be outstanding customer service. Your goal should be to create a "wow" experience which will help spread word of mouth.

To explain, what I mean by "wow" experience, I want to share a success email we received:

Subject: RE: iPad Air Berlin cover - kavaj.com
To: "KAVAJ.com | Service" <service@kavaj.com>

Dear Tom

Thank you for your prompt reply to my email.

I do not believe I have ever received such amazing customer service, I knew that the reputation of Kavaj was good but you have surpassed anything that I could have expected. Well done!

I am looking forward to my replacement cover from Amazon, in the meantime I have attached some photographs that will hopefully help you and you quality control team.

Our company is planning to order the iPad pro for our management team when it released and I will have no hesitation in recommending your covers.

Thanks

Again

Steve

We not only exceeded his expectation but we "surpassed anything that I could have expected!" In the end, he helped us fix the issue by sending us images and he will recommend our iPad Pro cases to his management team. This how you turn a negative into a positive.

START YOUR CUSTOMER SERVICE ON YOUR AMAZON PRODUCT PAGE.

This is the place where all your customers start their customer journey, read reviews, ask questions, check out your seller feedback and finally click the "Add to Cart" button. I recommend implementing a daily routine for your product pages including the following actions:

- Comment on negative product reviews and offer instant help
- Answer questions in the Q&A section
- Manage your seller feedback actively

ANSWER YOUR CUSTOMERS FAST AND BE GENEROUS.

The 2nd pillar of your customer service is email. You must answer all emails within 24 hours or faster and strive to resolve every customer service issue in a single communication.

I recommend to apply the following four principles:

- Answer all emails within 24 hours
- Provide a solution in your first reply
- Make it simple for your customer
- Be generous

BE RESPONSIVE ON YOUR SOCIAL MEDIA CHANNELS.

Your customers will talk about or to you and they expect you to engage with them on their favorite social media channel. We recommend using Facebook and Twitter as your first customer service channels. You can exceed expectations here and "wow" your customers if you reply to all questions within an hour.

We also recommend creating a FAQ section on your website that answers common questions. Finally, offer an easy-to-use contact form on your website.

Go International

One final note on your Amazon strategy:

> **This entire process works the same worldwide and the potential is huge.**

More than 300 million active customers are waiting for you. As a German company, we started out in Germany, which is still our biggest market. With Fulfilment by Amazon, it has never been easier to sell your products worldwide. You can see screenshots below of one of our iPad cases, which we sell in the U.S., U.K., Germany, and Japan.

Final Word

What are you waiting for? Selling on Amazon worldwide has never been easier. Apply the strategies mentioned in this guide and get started.

For the final time, always remember that your ultimate goal on Amazon is to get your product on page one of Amazon search results to benefit from the organic sales of the massive Amazon customer base.

From our eight years experience, the best way to achieve this is to focus on generating sales, getting authentic product reviews and providing outstanding customer service.

Most importantly, GET STARTED TODAY and TAKE ACTION NOW!

13 Amazon Revenue Calculator: Fees, Metrics & More

Lauren Shepherd, Senior Marketing Manager, Teikametrics

As an Amazon seller, you need to ask yourself one important question: "Is my Amazon business profitable?" The answer isn't as obvious as you might think.

> **Many sellers discover they are losing thousands of dollars every year.**

This is because they're using one-dimensional metrics to determine profitability. You can't tell a person's health by simply checking his heart rate, so why would you do the same for your Amazon business?

To effectively evaluate your profitability, you must analyze every aspect to determine your overall inventory health.

This is what we call the **Multidimensional Methodology.**

What is Multidimensional Methodology?

The Multidimensional Methodology will help you determine your profitability at the SKU level so you can make the most informed business decisions.

This may be regarding your:

- Pricing
- Inventory management and restocking
- Returns management
- Vendor negotiations

First, we'll go through the most effective methods to measure profitability on Amazon, and then we'll get into the specifics of how you can squeeze the most profit out of each dollar you invest.

Know Your Costs

> **If someone were to ask you if you knew your exact costs at the SKU level, would you be able to answer "yes"?**

Even the most organized sellers are missing out on hidden costs that are affecting their bottom line.

Let's get started with a review of the minimum list of costs that should be considered in your financial model:

- **Direct costs:** Your acquisition cost per SKU, including shipping.
- **Indirect (overhead) costs:** Warehouse costs, utilities, insurance, bookkeeping, payroll and benefits, business travel, corporate business tax, product samples, web development, etc.
- **Amazon fees:** Sales commission, FBA fees, FBA inbound shipping fees, commission on returned product, storage fees, return shipping costs (both from customer to Amazon fulfillment centers, and from fulfillment centers to you), and returns disposal costs.
- **Costs for handling returns once they are received:** What write-down or write-off costs do you have by not being able to sell these returned products as new condition products?

DETERMINING YOUR OVERHEAD ALLOCATION COST PER UNIT

To calculate this, add up your indirect costs over the past twelve months, and divide that sum by the number of units you sold in the last 12 months.

Use this number as a rule of thumb, as it should be consistent on a month to month basis.

$$\text{Overhead Allocation Cost} = \frac{\text{indirect cost (over trailing 12 months)}}{\text{sum of total \# of units sold (over trailing 12 months}}$$

You may want to refresh this calculation every 6 months.

Let's say, for example, that you calculated a $2.00 overhead allocation cost per unit sold. This is how much money you have spent on the sale of the item before you have purchased or sold it.

Typically, we see overhead allocation costs between $1 - $3 per unit.

If your overhead allocation cost is higher than that, it may be time to evaluate your individual business expenses and determine how to streamline your costs.

For example, let's say Kathy's Cat Toys is spending thousands of dollars on Amazon Sponsored Products every month to drive traffic to her Cozy Cat Castle.

However, **her return on her investment is three sales per month.**

Based on the high overhead allocation cost for that particular unit compared to her other SKUs, she will have to determine if that SKU is worth continuing to sell.

Take a Look at Your Amazon Fees

All Amazon fees can be pulled in one to two week time frames out of Seller Central **(Seller Central > Reports > Payments > All Statements View).**

Keep in mind your FBA fees will be higher for items that are heavy or large. Also, be sure to monitor any slow-moving SKUs, as stale inventory can cause you to rack up additional fees.

Lastly, while some of your expenses may be SKU specific, some are not. Once expenses are calculated by individual SKU, the remaining costs should be allocated across all units sold. This is a very simple approach to profitability calculations and will provide you the minimum amount of information you need to monitor your costs day-to-day, or month-by-month.

To summarize, let's review your costs:

- Wholesale cost
- Inbound/outbound shipping
- Amazon commissions
- FBA fees
- Overhead cost allocation
- Returns-related costs

Unfortunately, if you don't have a constant pulse on your profitability by SKU, it can be difficult to make the necessary changes to vendor negotiations, inventory management or product sourcing promptly.

By moving toward a model of profitability by SKU (updated every 3-6 months), having a decent understanding of the overhead allocation cost that you should be applying to all current sales, and knowing the impact of product returns on your SKU-level and overall profitability, you can become a smarter seller.

This knowledge will help inform and educate future buying decisions.

If Kathy's Cat Toys is selling a lightweight, feather toy that is incurring minimal FBA fees, has low overhead costs, and sells like hot cakes, Kathy knows to reorder that toy.

However, the Cozy Cat Castle that is heavy, large, and is slow-moving is a SKU that Kathy should consider to no longer purchase or even remove from FBA so as not to incur further fees.

A lot of smaller brands choose to track all of these calculations through spreadsheets, but this can be extremely inefficient and time consuming.

Most successful mid-market sellers decide to employ a third-party software to automate this process and help them determine their true profitability.

Identify Trends That Are Costing You Money

RETURNS

While some products may have a high return rate (e.g., 20% of orders are returned), you may easily be able to resell all of those items as 'new' condition a second time if a customer doesn't open or tamper with the product before returning it.

Other products may have low return rates, but are a complete write-off if returned (e.g., software, vitamins, underwear).

If you are forced to resell the SKU as 'used' following a return, there is a write-down cost incurred by not being able to generate the revenue you would have received were the item in 'new condition.'

For example, if you are selling an iPad and the customer chooses to return it, you would have to sell the item for a lower price as 'like new' or 'used.'

> **As products are returned, you should be tracking not only the proportion of each SKU being returned but also the cost per return regarding write-downs or write-offs.**

This can be found in Seller Central reports or automated through third-party software. It's crucial to monitor return rates and return-related costs because occasionally, those costs will actually be high enough to warrant removing the products from your catalog.

Alternatively, you may have the option to push part of that cost onto your distributor/supplier with whom you share the returns-related cost data. For example, let's say Molly's Marionettes have seen a large number of returns. After Molly does a returns analysis, she finds that she is losing money. Once she removes the problem product from her catalog, she sees a 10% increase in profit the next month.

STOCKOUTS

Inventory stockouts happen to even the most experienced Amazon sellers and have the potential to be one of the biggest leaks in your profitability bucket.

How much are inventory stockouts costing you?

Let's go over an example of just how much of an impact stockouts had on Steve's Sporting Goods.

> *Steve is an established Amazon seller with over 5,000 products and his top seller is a pair of high-end soccer cleats. The cleats have been flying off the shelves and are selling at an average of 60 units per month, with a profit of $50 per unit.*
>
> *On average, Steve is out of stock on these cleats an average of 2.5 days per month, equaling a loss of $1,500 in profit over the course of the year ((2.5 days x $50/unit) x 12 months in a year = $1,500). While this may not seem like a lot, let's consider Steve's business as a whole. Using the Pareto Principle, or the 80/20 rule, we can assume that 20% of Steve's inventory generates 80% of his profits, so 1,000 of his 5,000 SKUs. If we estimate that on average, his profit per SKU sold is $10 and he sells 10,000 of his top 20% of SKUs.*
>
> *If Steve were able to cut his average stockout time per month in half, he would make an additional $50,000 of profit each year.*

WHY STOCKOUTS HAPPEN AND HOW TO PREVENT THEM

Scenario 1: An Increase in Customer Demand

Some changes in demand will be unpredictable, like when Kate Middleton wears a particular dress (known as "the Kate Middleton Effect") and sales shoot through the roof.

How to Prevent this Stockout Scenario: Not all stockouts can be remedied with the same solution. First, take a look at the type of product you're selling.

Since the "Kate Middleton Effect" is hard to predict, the best solution is to build a buffer into your buying strategy to prepare for scenarios like these. Keep in mind that this strategy has drawbacks as well. If your product doesn't sell, you risk paying those pesky FBA storage fees.

Scenario 2: Annual Seasonal Variations

Every retailer knows that when spring begins, your winter boot sales become slower than molasses in January and your rain boots and sandals begin to fly off the shelves. For many sellers, this often results in stockouts.

How to Prevent this Stockout Scenario: If you are selling seasonal items, you'll want to monitor changes in your historical sales rank and stay on top of other factors, like weather patterns, to help predict inventory levels. This can be tracked through spreadsheets or third party software.

Scenario 3: Complications with Your Supplier

Occasionally, you will run into supplier issues that are outside of your control. For example, Nike decides to discontinue your best selling running shoe or your wholesaler ran out of stock.

How to Prevent This Stockout Scenario: Be your supplier's best customer and maintain open lines of communications with them at all times. This way, you can be alerted in advance to any changes in their product line or SKU volume and adapt your strategy accordingly.

Most importantly, you'll know if any of your best selling items are about to be discontinued, giving you the ability to buy up a bunch of extra inventory so you can continue to enjoy these sales for as long as possible.

Scenario 4: Changes in Demand Resulting from Competitior

There are two potential causes for this scenario:

- **Your Kitchen Aid blender has been struggling to sell for weeks and all the sales have gone to your competitor, Kelly's Kitchen Supplies**. All of a sudden, Kelly runs out of stock and you're the top seller on the listing. This causes demand of your blender to go through the roof and you are not able to keep up, causing you to go out of stock.
- **The opposite scenario happens when Amazon sees the success you are having with your Kitchen Aid blender and begins to sell the same SKU**. Now you are never able to win the Buy Box, no matter how low you go with your price.

How to Fix This Stockout Scenario: It's crucial to regularly monitor your sales volume and price changes to catch variations in sales velocity for your SKUs. This will help you catch the first cause as quickly as possible so you can adapt your strategy.

Depending on your competition, you may want to increase your price to get even more of a profit margin out of this temporary spike in sales. Competitors jumping on a listing is becoming more and more of a common occurrence. To properly prepare for this particular situation, always be diversifying and expanding your portfolio so that losing a few SKUs won't make or break your business.

The more diverse you are at the brand, supplier and SKU levels, the lower your risk. Always be scouting for new brands to sell so that if your best supplier begins to sell directly to Amazon or if your supplier cuts you off completely, you have more profitable products to rely on in your portfolio.

Know Your Metrics

Key Performance Indicators (KPIs) are crucial for the success of any business. These metrics can help you evaluate your success at reaching key targets, allow you to spot trends or problem areas, and assess your overall performance. They are used across all industries but are particularly useful for retail businesses. The most successful Amazon sellers know to segment their analysis by brands, suppliers and buyers, and review metrics for each of these areas at least once a week. Here are the most important KPIs to evaluate the health of your Amazon business:

INVENTORY TO SALES RATIO

Inventory value ÷ Revnue past 30 days

This key management metric covers multiple areas of your business. It indicates the overall health of your inventory, as well as highlighting your sell-through rate.

INVENTORY TURNS

Cost of goods sold ÷ Average inventory value

This ratio shows how many times a company's inventory is sold and replaced over a period of time. A low turnover rate implies poor sales and, therefore, excess inventory.

GROSS MARGIN RETURN ON INVESTMENT (GMROI)

Gross margin ÷ Average inventory cost

GMROI is a ratio used to evaluate inventory profitability. A ratio higher than one means you are selling the merchandise for more than the total cost it took to acquire it.

CASH TO CASH CYCLE

Days inventory outstanding + Days sales outstanding - Days payable outstanding

Cash to Cash Cycle measures the amount of time it takes for capital invested to go from cash to the production and sales process and then convert into cash again through sales. This metric looks at the amount of time needed to sell inventory, the amount of time needed to collect cash owed, and the length of time the company is afforded to pay its bills without incurring penalties.

The longer your cash to cash cycle is, the more time your cash flow is tied up. This means you are losing out on potentially more profitable investments.

DAYS OF INVENTORY (DOI)

Quality on hand ÷ Sales during periods ÷ Period

This KPI will help you see the average number of days an item is held in inventory before it is sold. It's extremely useful in determining order quantity to ensure you are not overstocking or stocking out of your inventory. Days of inventory (DOI) is much higher for companies not tracking KPIs.

Profitability Leaks

Tracking your metrics is key because the dollars are in the details. While these details may seem minute, when the mistakes add up they can make or break your business. Here are some commonly missed profitability leaks unique to Amazon sellers:

- **Returned items that are lost or damaged:** Occasionally, items returned by customers are either lost or damaged in transit and the seller of that item never receives it.
- **You don't receive your refunds:** When a customer returns one of your products to Amazon, Amazon immediately refunds the customer the amount they paid for the item. However, occasionally that refunded payment never makes it back to the seller's account.
- **Amazon does not receive your shipments in full:** It's common for parts of your shipment to get lost or damaged along the way to Amazon's fulfillment centers. It's crucial to confirm the SKUs you sent over to FBA match up with the shipment Amazon has received.
- **The SKU quantity sent from your vendor is incorrect:** Check, check and re-check again that the quantity you receive from your vendor is the same as the quantity you are expecting.

Now that you know about some of the most common profitability leaks and the key metrics you need to pay attention to in order to evaluate your true profitability, let's talk about how to squeeze the most out of each dollar you invest.

Use Your Profitability Analysis to Squeeze More Out of Your Dollar

VENDOR NEGOTIATION

Lay all of the facts out on the table and perform an audit on all of your suppliers. This will help you spot areas where you can negotiate to get better deals.

For example, the seller should be able to leverage their large sales volume and five-year relationship to negotiate better payment terms.

PRODUCT SOURCING

Now that you know your most profitable SKUs using the metrics we outlined, use your findings to inform your future buying decisions. Also, remember that the more diverse your portfolio is, the less risk you have of seeing a large drop-off in profit in case one of your product lines is discontinued or your brands go out of business.

HISTORICAL PROFITABILITY TRENDS

If you identify that your pink oven mitt sales have been decreasing over time, it's time to consider whether or not you want to reorder that product. Remember that all products have a lifecycle –– the key is to pay attention to trends.

CONSIDER THIRD PARTY SOLUTIONS

Seller Central's reports are often not thorough enough and spreadsheets can be a pain to update and manage. Save time by automating processes that can be more effectively managed by technology.

If you are interested in learning more about how you can automate the processes outlined above to identify your true profitability at the SKU level, contact the good folks over at Teikametrics. In the meantime, here's a full infographic view of how to measure your profitability.

HOW TO DETERMINE THE HEALTH OF YOUR
AMAZON BUSINESS
Introducing Multidimensional Methodology

Sounds boring, right? But what if we told you it could save you millions? Brands selling on Amazon are losing $$$$ by incorrectly calculating their profits. Here's how to determine your profitability on Amazon per SKU.

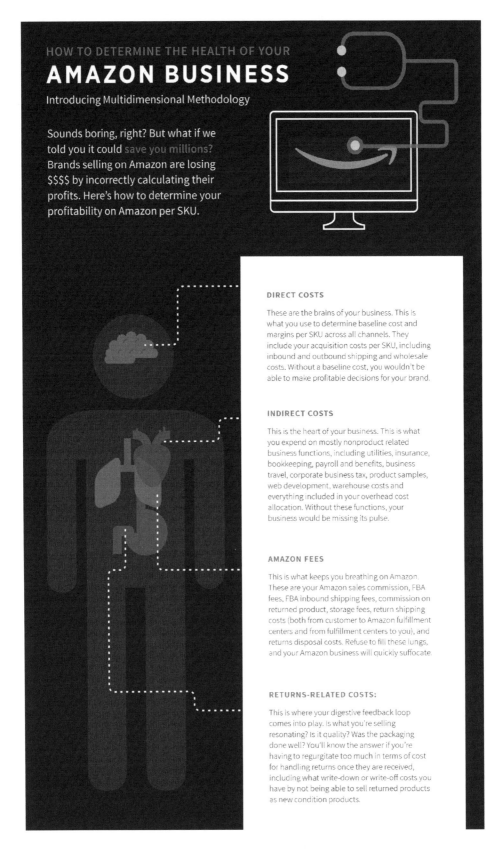

DIRECT COSTS

These are the brains of your business. This is what you use to determine baseline cost and margins per SKU across all channels. They include your acquisition costs per SKU, including inbound and outbound shipping and wholesale costs. Without a baseline cost, you wouldn't be able to make profitable decisions for your brand.

INDIRECT COSTS

This is the heart of your business. This is what you expend on mostly nonproduct related business functions, including utilities, insurance, bookkeeping, payroll and benefits, business travel, corporate business tax, product samples, web development, warehouse costs and everything included in your overhead cost allocation. Without these functions, your business would be missing its pulse.

AMAZON FEES

This is what keeps you breathing on Amazon. These are your Amazon sales commission, FBA fees, FBA inbound shipping fees, commission on returned product, storage fees, return shipping costs (both from customer to Amazon fulfillment centers and from fulfillment centers to you), and returns disposal costs. Refuse to fill these lungs, and your Amazon business will quickly suffocate.

RETURNS-RELATED COSTS:

This is where your digestive feedback loop comes into play. Is what you're selling resonating? Is it quality? Was the packaging done well? You'll know the answer if you're having to regurgitate too much in terms of cost for handling returns once they are received, including what write-down or write-off costs you have by not being able to sell returned products as new condition products.

HOW TO PERFORM REGULAR SELF CHECKUPS

Here's what to measure to have a pulse on your profitability per SKU. Are you in the green?

INVENTORY TO SALES COSTS

Indicates overall health of your inventory, as well as highlighting your sell through rate.

$$\frac{\text{Inventory Value}}{\text{Revenue past 30 days}}$$

GROSS MARGIN RETURN ON INVESTMENT

A ratio higher than 1 means you are selling the merchandise for more than the total cost it took to acquire it.

$$\frac{\text{Gross margin}}{\text{Average inventory cost}}$$

INVENTORY TURNS

A low turnover rate implies poor sales and, therefore, excess inventory.

$$\frac{\text{Cost of goods sold}}{\text{Average inventory value}}$$

CASH TO CASH CYCLE

The longer your cash to cash cycle is, the more time your cash flow is tied up. This means you are losing out on potentially more profitable investments.

Days inventory outstanding + Days sales outstanding + Days payable outstanding

ANNUAL CHECKUP

Most business come in at $1-$3 per unit. If you are higher, evaluate how to streamline your overhead costs.

OVERHEAD ALLOCATION COST =

$$\text{Overhead Allocation Cost} = \frac{\text{indirect costs (over trailing 12 months)}}{\text{sum of total \# of units sold (over trailing 12 months)}}$$

DANGER AHEAD!

Potential profitability leaks and negative trends.

RETURNED ITEMS THAT ARE LOST OR DAMAGED

Occasionally, items returned by customers are either lost or damaged in transit and the seller of that item never receives it.

THE SKU QUANTITY SENT FROM YOUR VENDOR IS INCORRECT

Check, check and re-check again that the quantity you receive from your vendor is the same as the quantity you are expecting.

AMAZON DOES NOT RECEIVE YOUR SHIPMENTS IN FULL

It's common for parts of your shipment to get lost or damaged along the way to Amazon's fulfillment centers. It's crucial to confirm the SKUs you sent over to FBA match up with the shipment Amazon has received.

YOU DON'T RECEIVE YOUR REFUNDS

When a customer returns one of your products to Amazon, Amazon immediately refunds the customer the amount they paid for the item. However, occasionally that refunded payment never makes it back to the seller's account.

14

How to Make $5,000 an Hour Selling on Amazon

Andrew Tjernlund, Multi-million Dollar Amazon Seller and Amazon Selling Consultant

I get it.

> **You don't understand the complexity that is selling on Amazon, and you don't have time to learn it.**

Don't worry –– I have it covered.

I've sold tens of millions both on Amazon as a third party seller and tens of millions more directly to Amazon. Those millions sold have been made selling a variety of products, among various industries, at a mix of price points and using several different methods.

However, the basic principles are universal, so while **I can't guarantee you a sales volume on Amazon**, I can stand behind a productivity number: $5,000 in sales for every hour you spend on Amazon activities.

So how can you grow your business to make serious money on Amazon? Let's dive into some straight talk.

Get Enthusiastic

Amazon is the future. It's time to get on board and excited about it. To do that, don't just make Amazon part of a growth strategy. Make it the growth strategy for your business. I've worked with an old fashioned manufacturer that has been in business for several generations. **Within 18 months they were selling more on Amazon than through their traditional channels.**

How did they do it? They didn't mess around when it came to selling on Amazon. They tossed their whole product line on Amazon, identified the services they needed to outsource and created new internal processes specifically for Amazon.

Here's the same checklist they used:

1. Identify what items make sense for you to sell on/to Amazon.
2. Check if the items are already sold on Amazon.
   a. Free tools like Keepa.com can help you gauge if the items have already been sold by Amazon Retail at some point.
3. Compile the necessary information to submit those items to Amazon
   a. Perhaps use existing Amazon listings for your product
   b. Collect pictures, feature data and descriptions
4. Identify the processes an Amazon order will follow
5. Search for and implement software services that simplify these steps
6. Recruit Virtual Assistants for any tasks that are not already performed and core to your business
7. Create and document processes that absolutely cannot be done within 4 and 5
8. Submit the product data to Amazon (Seller Central or Vendor Express)
9. Process orders
10. Make improvements to 4, 5 and 6 as necessary

Amazon is not overly complicated and does not have to be your biggest competitor. In fact, it can be your initial parlay into household name status, and multi-million dollar sales.

Sell Directly to Amazon

Don't try to beat Amazon at its own game.

> **Amazon is growing its direct catalog, so swim with the tide -- not against it.**

Aside from Amazon becoming your customer instead of your competitor, selling directly to Amazon eliminates the job new sellers are worst at, i.e. **forecasting and marketing your product become Amazon's duty.**

Editor's Note: The promotion of your products remains your brand's responsibility unless you pay Amazon to do it for you. According to James Thomson, former head of Selling on Amazon, "If you sell to Amazon, Amazon doesn't promote anything unless you step up and pay big marketing dollars. Promoting your brand remains your responsibility."

Also, many items sold by Amazon sell for more and faster, all things being equal. There will be a margin difference for FBA sellers that are not competing against Amazon here.

> **In other words, selling unique goods on Amazon currently not already sold there is how you make the most margin.**

Re-read the chapter about why re-selling is the least practical method to Amazon success to understand why this is.

So, let's see: selling directly to Amazon puts you on the right side of the future, is easier and leads to more sales. Keep in mind; this doesn't mean it is right for everyone, but it certainly is an option.

Sell on Amazon Yourself

This isn't [necessarily] a contradiction to the previous section. Start by selling yourself on Amazon if you find it easier to get up and going, or use this to complement your sales to Amazon.

Selling on Amazon along with selling to Amazon keeps Amazon honest and doesn't allow the whims of their algorithm to lead to stockouts of your products.

Selling to Amazon also allows you to jump start sales of new products by giving Amazon's bots the confidence they need to start bringing it in themselves.

Editor's Note: This practice is not recommended for most sellers, especially sellers that are novice to selling on Amazon. Consult an Amazon consultant before using this method.

A CASE STUDY: HOW TO SELL TO — AND ON — AMAZON

A sheet metal factory in the industrial space wanted to come out with a line of consumer products to sell on Amazon.

Based on some cursory searches on Amazon for sheet metal products and knowing the limits of their machinery, they created a simple folding work bench to be used in congested garages and sheds.

It was made with the machines they already had, hardware they were already buying and sheet metal they already stocked.

Their initial production run was four units. **Yup, four.**

The total cost of labor and materials was less than most people's weekly grocery bill. They put up an Amazon listing and sold two units in the first week.

After that first week and with lifetime sales of only two units, the sellers, who had created an account to sell directly to Amazon, offered the product directly to Amazon.

The price offered to Amazon was similar to the net amount the company received from Amazon when selling through Seller Central.

Since selling commission and shipping costs were no longer part of the equation, the sellers could sell their product to Amazon for significantly less than $149.95 without actually cutting into their margin.

Within a week of submitting the product, the company received an order from Amazon for five units.

Although Amazon's Order Had Not Yet Shipped They Still Promoted the Product

Despite only two sales, the product moved to the third result in relevant keywords, in a similar position to items with as many as 138 reviews.

Of course, a sale of five items to Amazon is small time, but the idea of going from product concept to the top of the rankings on Amazon in a few weeks is possible. **It is highly unusual, but it is doable.**

Use Amazon Cleverly

Once you have become familiar with the inner workings of Amazon, you should take a step back. Look at your business with just Amazon in mind and figure out which services or methods provide you the most benefit.

LEVEL 1: DROPSHIPPING WITH FBM

Adding non-stock or custom items to Amazon and then drop shipping to customers can add to your revenue, but it can also help reveal new trends or overlooked items that should be stocked as part of a standard offering.

If you are setting up to dropship already, there is nothing to lose. All costs, including Amazon's, are variable and since items can be added to Amazon with little set up, even the administrative hassle is minimal.

Think this seller has 2,000 sitting on a shelf? No, but if someone preferred to buy on Amazon, they would get the sale.

Amazon allows this seller to be available to millions of shoppers and only produce an item once it has actually been sold.

PRICE DISCRIMINATION

Not sure how to price your items, especially newly launched products?

> # Play around by adjusting the price on Amazon to see what the effect has on volume.

Because pricing is relatively instantaneous, it is possible to offer a product at a variety of different price points so that in a few days or weeks a brand or retailer has a better idea of the optimal price. This can be helpful because price tags and price sheets have a perceived permanency in the minds of consumers, but online prices do not.

Take advantage of this to test prices for better Amazon margins or velocities, and to optimize those numbers for sales outside of Amazon, like in a retail store or website.

If I didn't know any better, I would think that the top two organic results for "Pour Over Coffee Stand" were really the same product sold at two different prices to test two different pricing strategies.

Hint: they are.

LEVEL 2: FBA FOR ITEMS SOLD OUTSIDE OF AMAZON

FBA is simply just that. Items are fulfilled by Amazon. There is the implication that these items are likely also sold on Amazon, but that does not have to be the case.

Many sellers use Amazon's fulfillment services to pick, pack and ship items that were sold elsewhere like a retail or online store. This is done even when they may have stock in their warehouse.

Amazon's shipping rates with the major carriers are so low that, even with the additional charges for picking and packing, their total shipment cost can be lower than negotiated carrier rates for many mid-market firms. This can be true even for shipments within a company's own state.

Editor's Note: Sellers often use this service so they don't have to split inventory for Amazon and non-Amazon channels. James Thomson, former head of Selling on Amazon warns, "If you use FBA to fulfill orders outside of Amazon (called multi-channel fulfillment), Amazon raises the shipping costs, and you aren't likely to see much cost saving at all."

Additionally, Amazon has extremely low 2-Day and Next Day rates, so during the end of the Christmas season, many sellers are able to offer quick shipping for reasonable prices by leveraging Amazon's buying power.

COST TO SHIP FROM A WAREHOUSE COMPARED TO AMAZON SHIPPING THE SAME ITEM

Why not have Amazon ship every unit if you can save 25% in shipping fees, the cost of labor and materials by having them do everything?

Here's an example from my own product set.

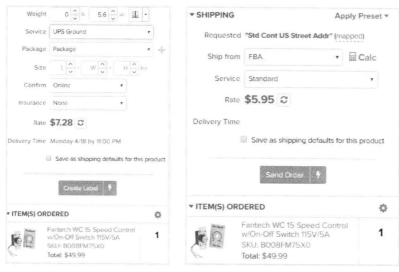

OFFERING COMPETITIVE PRODUCTS

Odds are that you have competition -- and that they are pretty successful, too. Why not cash in on their sales and success by offering their products on Amazon as well? Not only might you get better insight into their sales numbers and product features, but you'll be getting paid to do it.

More sincerely, you probably have holes in your product line:

- You don't carry a certain color
- They have metric versions you don't
- They have a unit that sells for under $100 and your cheapest offering is $119.

Even if you don't offer the whole line, you may be able to generate more sales on your own site and on Amazon by extending your product line to include items your competitors offer for which you don't have a substitute.

Look at these four different clothes dryer lint traps from four different manufacturers. The only way to make money off of every version sold on Amazon is two win the Buy Box for each one like the seller below, Professional Grade Products.

LEVEL 3: AMAZON PRIVATE LABE|

Consider offering a line of products on Amazon that is only available on Amazon.

What makes a product unique, technically?

> ## To Amazon, a unique UPC. To most customers, a specific model number

That's it. Not a different patent number, manufacturer or even color. Whether it is a specific bundle or the same item as normally available, but in a different box, many sellers see the best results by having a unique offering on Amazon. Often, dealers or brands are only concerned about their products and not a brand's or reseller's version of a similar product.

As an example, Amazon selling brand Vortex is selling the same product, but at a different price point to try to be true to their main "premium" brand, but also get more volume through a generic brand item.

Just "Amazon" it.

THE HUGE OPPORTUNITIES IN PRIVATE LABELING ON AMAZON

In the late 2000's, and continuing on today to a degree, most brands that had traditionally dominated big box retail channels shied away from selling on Amazon. They feared having their items sold on Amazon would diminish their brand and annoy their existing retail partners.

This led to holes in Amazon's catalog in many high velocity categories because the brands that dominated that space everywhere else were not represented on Amazon.

Naturally, new "Amazon Only" brands are continually created to fill that space.

> ## Can you create the top brand on the world's top marketplace? We are in a rare moment in time when you really might be able to.

monthly sales volume. Use this to find new products or estimate your market share.

IF NO ONE HAS CREATED A PROGRAM FOR A COMPUTER TO USE (BASED ON #1), PERHAPS IT IS BECAUSE THAT TASK ISN'T WORTH DOING IN THE FIRST PLACE.

Many new sellers make the mistake of focusing on the small stuff. They are so eager to succeed on Amazon that they put all their effort into fine tuning a single or handful of listings even though it makes almost no difference to the customer.

There is no software program that reshuffles your product images in different orders, rearranges your bullet points and A/B tests "cozy" vs "comfy" as adjectives in your listing title. Yes, you want good listings with beautiful pictures. You want to generate some reviews.

But, with competition always on the same page and just a click away, **remember that five minutes negotiating a better price with your supplier or using a cheaper shipping service is more valuable than spending 100 hours perfecting an Amazon listing.**

CASE STUDY OF PRIORITIES IN THE WRONG PLACE

The Search: Silicone Pour Over Dripper

The top result spent five minutes creating a listing. They did not pay a service for any product reviews, edit their listing to test different keywords, or frankly, give it a second thought once they sent in their inventory to Amazon. The picture, title, bullets and description are acceptable. Simple as that.

What they did do, however, was commit to 1000 units out of the gate and negotiate exceptionally good pricing so that they could afford to sell it for a few cents cheaper than their competition (See the 4th and 5th items that are from the same manufacturer in China).

Also, unlike those listings appearing below the POVA one, no reviews were paid for, so there was no need to factor in hundreds of giveaways and service fees into the price.

Who knew people shopped based on cost alone?

Alternatively, see page 8 of the same search -- a yellow version of the exact item from a different seller with 17 subsidized product reviews, a bunch of staged photos, a convoluted title (it's not a filter after all) and for what?

The second mantra put in different terms could be, "Are you productive or busy?"

Are you genuinely adding value to or eliminating waste within the process (like using Amazon integrated

> **Make no mistake; Amazon doesn't want to be tricked, so even something that works, for now, may not work in the future.**

Stick with proven productivity enhancers like the software programs out there for sellers like you.

IF A TASK CAN'T BE DONE BETTER BY A COMPUTER, BUT STILL IS WORTH DOING THEN THERE ARE LIKELY PEOPLE SPECIALIZING IN THAT TASK THAT CAN DO IT MORE EFFECTIVELY THAN YOU.

Listen, a lot of Amazon experts and courses will emphasize the value of pictures, bullet points, and listing titles. I am not saying those are not important.

They are, as is:

- Customer service
- Compliance
- Advertising
- Listing management.

You need to make sure all of these things get done and are done well. But, you certainly don't have to do them yourself. Use these services to outsource the work.

FIVERR

Fiverr is easy to set up, has great results and is only $5.

- Need the backgrounds removed for some product shots? 5 bucks.
- Want someone to research relevant keywords and add them to your listing? Just 5 dollars.
- Need someone to scrape data from your site to add to your Amazon listing? $5.

Editor's Note: This site also has a bad rap for having been the destination to get fake product reviews. Do not pay for product reviews on Amazon.

UPWORK

Thousands of people with Amazon experience are available for custom jobs through Upwork. The general process is:

1. Search for people with a particular skill set or simply post a job description and wait on applicants –– usually you will have two dozen within 24 hours.
2. Select candidates, submit any interview questions
3. Choose a person to hire

There are extensive reviews on most freelancers and Upwork has programs that allow you to monitor progress and keep the workers honest. Many are well-versed in Amazon-specific tasks and can be hired for a single job or on an ongoing basis.

Users can create a stable of freelancers that have delivered well in the past, helping you to build a network that is more and more efficient over time. The productivity gains here are substantial.

FREEEUP

Don't have time even to worry about hiring people for specific Amazon activities? Of course not, you have been reciting your mantras.

Freeeup was created by an Amazon expert who created a corral of hundreds of Upwork freelancers. Freeeup assigns and manages your team freelancers based on the complexity of the Amazon services.

If you need to create listings, fulfill orders, advise on reorders and handle customer service, you can try to recruit all those people or just send a message to Freeeup and they will handle it all.

CONSULTANTS

Software and outsourcing services can help you execute your plan, but what if you need help developing your plan? This book should give you a working knowledge of how to concoct an Amazon strategy, but invariably each business has its complexities and complications.

There are a handful of good Facebook groups and message boards, but for tailor-made solutions, consider reaching out to someone who walks the walk.

15 The 4 Secrets to Long-Term Amazon Success [Including FBA]

Yaffa Klugerman, Content Manager, Feedvisor

Long-term success on Amazon comes down to four key processes:

1. Competitive review
2. SKU strategy
3. Inclusion in FBA
4. Repricing.

For brands already selling on Amazon, mastering these four areas will allow you to continually improve your rankings, your product offering and your revenue from Amazon as a channel. Here's how to think through each aspect and bring your brand to world-class status on Amazon.

Be a Strategic Purchaser

As you expand your inventory of ASINs (Amazon Standard Identification Number), you'll want to make sure that each purchase was made thoughtfully and logically. It's key to conduct research into potential merchandise ahead of buying, lest you end up with non-competitive, unreliable or otherwise problematic stock that you'll be forced to liquidate earlier than planned.

Below are key elements to consider when making purchasing decisions:

1. SALES RANK

There are two types of ASINs you should be on the lookout for:

1. Those with an extremely high ranking
2. Those with no ranking at all.

A high ranking ASIN will allow you to sell an item that's already popular with buyers, making it a safe bet, while a very low (or non-existent) ranking could open up new markets and establish you as the dominant seller.

2. PRODUCT REVIEWS

A lot of great customer reviews are a good sign about an ASIN. Pay attention to them. On the other hand, don't let one or two negative reviews spoil the whole bunch. Often, outliers may be irrelevant to the product, such as when the product description wasn't read carefully.

3. FBA STATUS

A product without FBA offerings presents a perfect window of opportunity if you are an FBA seller. But be careful. **Ask yourself why that ASIN isn't already being sold through FBA.** In some cases, it could be deemed hazardous and forbidden for FBA.

4.PRICE FLUCTUATIONS

Check out the ASIN's history. A history of dramatic leaps and plummets may indicate price wars, which you would be wise to avoid.

5. THE COMPETITION

It's important to consider how many sellers are sitting on an ASIN, which Amazon refers to as "offer depth." Purchasing an ASIN that lacks offer depth is an easy way to establish yourself as the main seller, but an ASIN with dozens of sellers can indicate that there is enough demand for that product that you could still stand a chance of getting a piece of that pie.

6. AMAZON SEARCH PLACEMENT

Amazon Search results will indicate whether the ASIN is high or low ranking. Both situations present unique opportunities and challenges — it all depends on how you want to strategize.

A high-ranking ASIN allows you to capitalize on the profitability of an ASIN whose success is already proven. And a low-ranking ASIN provides the opportunity to expand into new territory as the main seller.

7. ITEM CATEGORIES

You're probably already thinking in terms of item categories. Maybe you specialize in one particular area, and it's working well so far. Don't be afraid to venture into other categories, as long as you can back up your reasons for expanding. It may be easier to start by expanding into a related category at the beginning.

Apply a Unique Strategy for Each ASIN

Your company is growing rapidly, and it's now harder than ever to strategize for each ASIN individually. At the same time, you understand that applying a one-size-fits-all solution is not the answer. The most efficient and effective way to handle this is by focusing your efforts on your best selling items. Here's our recommended four-step process, and the questions you should be asking yourself at during each step.

1. CHOOSE A PROFIT MARGIN STRATEGY

- Are you operating a high- or low-profit margin business?
- Do you expect this to change or stay the same?

Understanding your big picture outlook is vital for all subsequent decisions.

2. UNDERSTAND REPLENISHMENT

- What is the sales cycle for the item?
- Is it a perennial best-seller that requires constant replenishment, or a seasonal success that functions on a different cycle?

3. ASSESS THE ASIN'S SEASONALITY

- Is this ASIN meant to sell out in a short cycle, or a longer one?

This is related to the previous point about replenishment.

4. BE AWARE OF LIQUIDATION NEEDS

If you're an FBA seller, you need to take into account that Amazon charges extra fees for items held in storage for over six months. Start the liquidation process ahead of time so you don't get hit with these fees. If an item's not selling, you may need to lower the price or have it returned to you.

Fulfillment Methods: FBA and SFP

There are two great fulfillment options for sellers wanting to scale their business:
- Fulfillment by Amazon (FBA)
- Fulfillment by Merchant (FBM)

Each has its own unique features and benefits.

SCALING WITH FBA

Fulfillment by Amazon (FBA) allows third-party Amazon sellers to delegate their packing, shipping and customer service process to Amazon's fulfillment centers, rather than handle logistics from their own home or office.

This method offers numerous benefits.

- **It frees up your time,** allowing you to focus on expanding your business and strategizing on items. You won't have to spread yourself thin or take on more employees — Amazon has its own well-oiled machine to handle the day-to-day aspects of running a business for you. In fact, FBA sellers received 33% less negative feedback than Fulfillment by Merchant (FBM) sellers.
- **As an FBA seller,** your products are automatically Prime eligible. When you consider the fact that 80 million Americans are Prime customers, this means you'll gain access to a wider range of buyers than you would have otherwise.

Here is a full list of FBA pros and cons.

FBA PROS:

- Prime eligibility
- Hands off fulfillment
- Buy box advantages
- Multi-channel fulfillment Lower shipping rates

FBA CONS:

- Additional fees
- Limited access to inventory
- Preparing product
- Pricey multi-channel fulfillment
- Tax obligations

FULFILLED-BY-MERCHANT (FBM)

FBM is a relatively new option that will allow you to fulfill orders yourself, while still receiving the same benefits of Amazon Prime that FBA sellers have access to.

Only top-performing, highly reliable sellers are eligible for this method. It's ideal for businesses who carry a lot of heavy items, who would otherwise be subject to FBA's overweight fees. Here's a full list of FBM pros and cons.

FBM PROS:

- Hands-on fulfillment
- Opportunity for Prime

- Fewer Amazon Fees
- Slightly higher margins

FBM CONS:

- More responsibility
- Not automatically Prime eligible
- Overhead costs
- Potentially lower conversions
- Elusive Buy Box

Choose the Right Repricer

As your business expands, the question is not whether you need to invest in a repricer — after all, **60% of high-grossing Amazon sellers (with a revenue of $2.5M- $10M) use one**, which is a good indicator of their importance. The question now becomes, which repricer is the right fit for you?

1. MANUAL REPRICING

Manual repricing isn't really a repricer since all it means is manually adjusting the prices on your ASINs yourself, one by one. The most basic form of setting prices, this method is best left to smaller sellers who have a manageable inventory, and limited funds to spend on technological solutions.

Since you are trying to build a multimillion dollar business, you're ready to move on from manually setting your prices, if you haven't already.

2. RULE-BASED REPRICING

Rule-based repricing in the most common repricing tool used by Amazon sellers.

> **You set a price-related rule — say, to be in the lowest 10% of sellers — and the software reprices according to your competition.**

One of the biggest problems with this type of repricer is that it feeds price wars, ultimately eroding your profit.

And it's especially short-sighted for sellers with high customer satisfaction ratings, who can often price higher than the competition and still win the Buy Box.

And it's especially short-sighted for sellers with high customer satisfaction ratings, who can often price higher than the competition and still win the Buy Box.

3. ALGORITHMIC REPRICING

Like rule-based repricing, algorithmic repricing is a tool that aims to automate your repricing process. But the similarities end there.

> **Algorithmic repricing, unlike rule-based, evaluates a whole host of seller performance metrics that go into winning the Buy Box using Big Data.**

This allows for highly accurate and profit-maximizing results. You won't have to worry about being priced down or leaving money on the table.

As you grow, investing in an algorithmic repricer — which comes with a higher upfront cost — will earn you more than you could have otherwise.

16

47 Essential Selling on Amazon Tips to Grow Sales and Win Market Share

Tracey Wallace, Editor-in-Chief, BigCommerce

Fifty-five percent of all online product searches begin on Amazon. Last year, the retail giant surpassed $107 billion in total sales. That is over $12,000,000 in sales every hour on average.

Amazon Prime alone boasts over 54 million members and counting. If Prime were a country, it would have 8,000,000 more people than Spain and be the 27th most populous in the world. Those are just Amazon Prime members. These mind-blowing stats are indicative of an undeniable fact: Amazon isn't going anywhere.

Many online sellers fear that Amazon is going to cut into their profit margins and inhibit — or outright squash — growth. And let's be honest: depending on your business model, those fears can be justified. But Amazon's dominance offers an upside that is proving lucrative for savvy ecommerce pros who have figured out how to make Amazon work for, not against them.

Amazon's control of market and mindshare isn't a closed ecosystem — they make it quite possible to leverage their advantages for your own business. You simply have to know how to play the game. That's why we rounded up these 45 experts who know how to win on Amazon best and have been doing so for years. Expedite your learning on selling on Amazon by tapping into their expertise below.

David Tendrich, CEO & Co-Founder, Reliable PSD

"Get. More. Reviews. I don't care how many you have. Get more."

People buy the product on Amazon that has the most positive reviews. When we're scared about making a decision, our brain falls back to certain factors and uses that limited information to make a decision. That first factor we fall back on is social proof.

We look around at everyone else and see what they think is a good idea. If a product has 10x more reviews than other products - we literally have to resist our biology to buy a different one that has less reviews and therefore more risk. So get reviews. Give away as many of your product as you have to in exchange for fair and honest reviews.

Bill Widmer, Ecommerce SEO & Content Marketing Consultant

"Write long, detailed product descriptions. At least 1,000 words."

 Not just fluff, either - add LSI keywords. Again, keyword research is CRITICAL here.

Daniel Wallock, Marketing Strategist, Wallock Media

"Don't just be an Amazon brand."

I mean that just because you're selling on Amazon doesn't mean that you can't promote the products with content, influencer campaigns, and get your products featured in the press. If your looking to increase sales on Amazon, I would look away from paid advertising and instead look at using inbound marketing tactics to traffic to your products. You can drive hundreds of visitors per day to your Amazon store or product pages just by creating a strong presence on niche forum sites, Facebook groups, and other social media channels.

Kaleigh Moore, Freelance Writer

"Build up positive reviews –– and incentivize customer ratings if you have to."

These are so important and can make or break a sale, not to mention the impact they have on ranking within the platform.

Ross Simmonds, Founder, Foundation Marketing

"Invest in quality product shots."

While it's always important to understand the value of optimizing for search rankings and getting positive reviews –– first impressions matter on Amazon. The number of new entrants into every category is through the roof. If you want to stand out, it's time to invest in not only building your own brand to help support an increased amount of search but also time to invest in high quality visuals to give a quality first impression.

Rupert Cross, Digital Director, 5874

"Don't compete on price – it's a race to the bottom and it's easy to become a busy fool."

Instead, focus on improving your rating by responding to all of the messages that matter as this a sure-fire way to ensure customers value you as a seller and choose you over somebody else. Sync your stock to avoid overselling.

Donald Pettit, Sales & Partners Manager, SalesWarp

"If you're looking to expand sales on Amazon, do it carefully. "

Make sure you have the bandwidth and necessary resources to take on additional orders. For example, an inventory management system can help prevent overselling items, and order management systems can help ensure timely deliveries.

Stock-outs and late deliveries can result in poor customer reviews, or a suspended Amazon account.

Additionally, try partnering with other brands and use Amazon as a laboratory for new offerings. For example, an apparel retailer partnering with smaller universities to offer branded products on Amazon that customers couldn't find elsewhere

Eric Carlson, Co-Founder, 10X Factory

If you have a lead on your list that hasn't bought from you ever and is older than 60 days old, DO THIS.

1. Send them a promotion for Amazon
2. Sync them with a Facebook custom audience.
3. Then, send clicks to your products on Amazon.

This is a WARM audience, but an audience that might not trust your website enough to buy from but likely will trust amazon.

David Feng, Co-Founder and Head of Product, Reamaze

"Amazon is a reviews-driven ecosystem."

It's vitally important to solicit for reviews effectively and reward customers post-purchase for contributing. Brands should also invest in SEO optimization especially for Amazon as it's a highly competitive environment for pricing, descriptions, reviews, and alternative products.

Finally, you need to understand Amazon's pricing structure and adjust your pricing with it. For example, by offering a significant discount from time to time or running a daily deal can get you enough brand exposure and attract repeat buyers. That, combined with great reviews and optimized SEO you'll have a winning strategy.

Jason Boyce, Co-founder & CEO, Dazadi

"The Amazon Channel should have it's own team and it's own procedures within your organization."

With roughly half of the online market share in the USA, you just can't succeed on Amazon unless you have a dedicated team with dedicated time and expertise on this channel.

There is so much to unpack here that it would take a book to share everything, but focusing on the best-sellers on the Amazon product categories pages can help you know if your items are priced well enough to gain sales and profits.

Sweta Patel, Director of Demand Generation, Cognoa

"Nothing is more effective than reviews on other platforms."

When we were selling mobile device products on Amazon we created an ubiquitous effect by promoting our reviews on all of our other channels.
These channels include:

- Facebook
- Twitter
- Touch of Modern
- Ebay
- Other publications through the display network.

Brian Nolan, Co-founder & CEO, Sellbrite

"Sponsored Products are a great way to drive additional traffic to your Amazon listings."

You can significantly level the playing field in terms of visibility against long-established competitors.

Bill Bailey, CEO, Nodal Ninja

"FBA - Fulfilled by Amazon."

Amazon sells 24/7 and setting up a FBA account on products you know will sell well will certainly increase your sales. FBA comes at a higher cost so a little Googling prior to doing this is best advise.

Having an Amazon store as well will help to keep abreast of the competition which most likely is already selling on Amazon.

Annie Cushing, Founder, Annielytics

"Engage with reviewers in a helpful, non-defensive manner."

Reviews play a significant role in ranking on Amazon.

Aaron Houghton, Co-Founder and CEO, BoostSuite

"Use paid search promotions inside Amazon."

And use your brand name and best performing keywords from Google Adwords.

Harrison Dromgoole, Content Creator, Ordoro

"Focus on the buy box."

Unless you're selling truly unique products, you're likely competing with other sellers to be the merchant behind the "Add to Cart" button.

There are two big ways to get in Amazon's favor -- and, Amazon being Amazon, they center around shipping. Utilize Fulfillment By Amazon, their fulfillment service, to store and ship orders, and if you're quick-shipping, high-volume e-retailer, try to qualify for their Seller Fulfilled Prime program, which guarantees access to lucrative Prime customers.

Jordan Brannon, President and COO, Coalition Technologies

"There are a million review generation tips out there. Most of them will work at some level."

Beyond that, really consider promoting Amazon through marketing channels typically reserved for your own website.

Amazon listings can be SEO'd. They can be advertised using PPC. They can be promoted via email and social. Also make sure you're planning ways to segment Amazon sales away from other sales channels to avoid creating your own competition.

Emil Kristensen, co-founder & CMO, Sleeknote

The most important thing on Amazon is ratings.
Make sure to have an automated process for gathering ratings from your customers. The Amazon algorithm that determines search rankings is highly influenced by product ratings, which is why ratings should be of high priority for your brand.

Another way is to think of your Amazon product site as an SEO site. This means you should include relevant keywords in your copy but be careful of keyword stuffing because search engines penalize this.

Josh Mendelsohn, VP Marketing, Privy

"Product content is the key to success."

Following their best practices around descriptions, categories, titles, and A+ content will help you dominate search results.

Sammy Gibson, Director, Neon Poodle

"We need to do it!"

Amazon has only just arrived in Australia and at the moment we don't have a presence and we are potentially missing out on many orders and expansion. This will be our main focus in the coming months.

Daniel Townsend, Managing Director, Plum Tree Group

"With more than 2 million sellers worldwide selling on Amazon, gaining the necessary visibility to succeed can be difficult."

However, all hope isn't lost. Amazon's latest release, headline search ads, may help new and experienced sellers by putting their products front and center in Amazon search results. Headline search ads are pay-per-click ads that help sellers target customers based on specific search terms.

Once campaign parameters are set (keywords, bid amount, and daily budget), headline search ads appear at the top of search results - a powerful opportunity to outrank similar products (aka healthy competition), drive shoppers to your listings, and increase sales.

Brita Turbyfill, Gray Loon

"Unique products."

If you sell a variety of products, that may or may not be unique from your competition, focus on selling the more unique products on Amazon and building up your product reviews.

Once you have several products that have a lot of positive feedback, then even if you have other products that your competitors have, you may build more of a loyal following based on those few unique products.

Ryan Bemiller, Founder, Shopping Signals

"Understand that reviews and SEO play a large part in getting your product listings in front of more people."

Amazon is a search engine as much as it is a marketplace. People search for products on Amazon. And Amazon has ranking factors to help it determine which products to show, in which order, when someone performs a search.

So do some research on Amazon's SEO factors. Things like title, subtitle, description, questions and answers, and even pictures all factor in on how a product will rank. Pay attention to keywords that people will use to find your products, and look at what keywords your competitors are using.

Reviews also play a big part in your ranking on Amazon. The frequency and overall number of reviews you get will help Amazon determine your rank. Be careful not to break Amazon's terms of service with respect to soliciting reviews, but do try to solicit reviews. You'll need them. Especially early-on when you're trying to get some traction for a new product.

Peter Attia, Founder, Dicey Goblin

"The biggest tip I have for Amazon is try to tack on an extra item with your listing."

Normally if you're selling an item on Amazon, other sellers can be on that same listing. That means you're not guaranteed to get the sale for that item, especially if you're not the lowest price.

We skirted around this by selling board games with a simple extra dice bag or expansion for the game. This allowed us to have our own unique listing that would still show up for the main product in Amazon search. This gave us more flexibility with the price, because we weren't trying to compete with other sellers for the same item. Plus, every purchase that came through that listing, went straight to us.

James Thomson, Partner, Buy Box Experts

"Optimize your listings with proper images and content."

Those will help customers make better decisions.... only then should you be spending any money on advertising. Otherwise, you are spending money to drive traffic to poor listings..yikes!

Jan Lastuvka, CEO & Co-Founder, MonkeyData

"Sell with Fulfillment by Amazon (FBA)."

Not only does this reduce work in handling orders, FBA products will appear in Prime-filtered searches. Also, products which are Prime eligible have higher conversion rates than those that do not. On top of this, having FBA products will allow you to tag on to the success that Amazon has built with its brand and align your business to their reputation.

William Harris, Ecommerce Consultant, Elumynt

"Amazon has a lot of similarities to Google Shopping - they are keyword and price driven."

If you're doing well on Google Shopping, export the list of keywords and see what you're doing the best at - then use that to bid on those keywords on Amazon to get some initial traffic flowing through and see if those keywords are going to work on Amazon as well.

Chris Van Dusen, CEO, Parcon Media

"Use Amazon's Keyword Tool to optimize your copy around long-tail keywords that are less competitive."

Sell more through Amazon on your own site by using the pay with Amazon button. Consumers trust Amazon more than you and they have their credit card details already stored for easy checkout.

Larry Kim, Founder, Wordstream

"Diversify!"

They're not the most vendor-friendly platform and make changes from time to time that aren't in the best interests of sellers. Not saying Amazon isn't a big deal, just suggesting that Amazon should be just one pillar of four or more major channels including Facebook Ads and Google Ads –– and, of course, your own direct web storefront.

Andy Eastes, Founder and CEO, SKUVault

"Focus on decreasing inventory errors like mis-picks, mis-ships, and out-of-stocks."

Order & inventory accuracy, as well as fewer customer mishaps, are both highly determining factors for winning the Buy Box and gaining access to the Prime Merchant-Fulfilled program.

Brett Curry, CEO, OMG Commerce

"Get reviews! Quality and quantity are necessary."

It's also better to have a few not-so-great reviews mixed in as long as your overall rating is strong. It makes your listing look real.

If all you have is a few 5 star reviews, customers will assume it was you or your mom who reviewed your product. Several studies show that products with more reviews outperform products with fewer reviews, even if the product with fewer reviews has a slightly higher average rating.

More reviews = more confidence.

Michael Ugino, Co-founder, Sellbrite

"The #1 rule of retail economics will always be that you make your money on the buy."

Thus, driving additional sales, even at less than your target price, will allow you to ultimately buy more and lower your sourcing costs. The best way to drive additional sales on Amazon is by using a repricing tool (with price floor limits of course) to constantly fight for, and win, the buy box.

Aaron Agius, Managing Director, Louder Online

"Give Amazon's suggested PPC campaigns a try."

I've seen a number of clients test them compared to the campaigns they built themselves based on tons of keyword data, metrics, etc, and still have Amazon's auto-generated campaigns produce a higher ROI. If it works for your brand, that's time you can spend elsewhere.

Kunle Campbell, Founder, 2X Ecommerce

"Endeavor to own your brand and listings on Amazon."

Competing with other retailers (including Amazon) on price is almost always certainly a race to the bottom. A single product listing with 10 sellers means that sellers can only really differentiate themselves by price alone.

This is a dangerous position to be in as a retailer and in business. You may eventually sell at your desired target price, but this may mean making a trade off in keeping stock longer with reduced inventory turnover.

Jacob Firuta, Content Manager, LiveChat

"Reviews from past customers give you the credibility you wouldn't otherwise get."

It's an extra portion of word-of-mouth that boosts your offer. It's in your best interest to get as many of them as possible. Have a customer that's raving about a particular product? Ask them to provide a review. Happy customers won't mind and it can significantly increase the number of reviews you get.

Drew Sanocki, Private Equity Operating Partner, Empire Growth Group

"For direct-to-consumer players, think of Amazon as customer acquisition."

Choose some small AOV top sellers and make sure you put them on Amazon. Encourage follow-on purchases through your own site in order to capture more customer data, up-and cross-sell, and increase overall LTV.

Kevin Rizer, Host, Private Label Podcast

"Optimize your listing!"

Proper title, bullet points, description and great images can drastically improve your sales.

David Potts, Founder and CEO, SalesWarp

"Amazon rewards sellers who can ship quickly and accurately."

Our clients are, often, best of breed in their segments. They provide fast fulfillment and avoid oversells or cancellations, and as a result, Amazon rewards them with prime seller advantages.

Catalin Zorzini, Founder, Ecommerce-Platforms.com

"Selling more on Amazon all depends on how many quality reviews you receive."

The sales are obviously going to figure into how often your product shows up in search results as well. The only problem is that telling you to get more reviews and sales doesn't really help much. However, you'll notice that many reviews come in because of free products being given away.

You have the ability to locate some of the more influential reviewers on Amazon, then you can give them 99% discounts in exchange for a review. The cool part is that many of the people that complete these reviews are willing to write quite a bit about the product, so other customers receive better information.

Jason Dea, Director of Product Marketing, Intelex

"Try as best as you can to focus on your customer experience and conversion rates."

Although you're limited in what you can do on Amazon, anything you can do to optimize your marketplace listings for conversion will catch the eye of the Amazon search algorithms.

Dennis Yu, CTO, BlitzMetrics

"You can go with paid options, of course..."

But nothing beats working toward getting tons of legitimate 5 star reviews.

Danna Crawford, Owner, PowerSellingMom.com

"Include quality, accurate, detailed descriptions."

Buyers appreciate more than just the "pre-filled" descriptions of items.

Raheem Sardar, Founder & CEO, RewardCamp

"Use these tactics."

Sellers are able to successfully charge higher prices for the same product using the following tactics on Amazon:

1. Brand your product
2. Register your brand with Amazon

3. Use high quality images and videos
4. Use your branding on product images, packaging, description, title, etc, so that it stands out from the competition
5. Get lots of reviews

Justin Mares, Founder, FOMO

"Focus on reviews."

Positive reviews drive higher conversion rate and drive rankings. Email your customers after they purchase asking for Amazon reviews and watch your rankings go up!

Ned Nadima, Growth Manager, Rare.io

"Master the art of branding."

Whenever customers search for products on Amazon, the search engine displays many similar products. Understanding how to position your brand properly will help you stand out. This includes product pictures, pricing, product description, reviews, etc. In order to accomplish the feat, you must nail your target market. Deeply understand your target market and you will succeed.

Erik Qualman, #1 Best Selling Author, Equalman.com

"The key on Amazon for their search algorithm."

Also, influencing buyers is to have good ratings and reviews around your product. There are many ways to accomplish this, but one critical thing to do is to comment/reply to all your current reviews.

Rieva Lesonsky, CEO, GrowBiz Media/SmallBizDaily.com

"Amazon also allows you to sell your service on Amazon."

When people buy products, your service can be offered as an add-on and everything is handled through Amazon.

This is something I know from personal experience. We bought a ceiling fan and at the same time I bought the installation from a local small company. Payment was handled through Amazon and then the company called me to set up an appointment.

Appendix

From our Guide to Selling on Amazon, you fully understand the vast potential of tapping into Amazon's 304 million (and growing) active user base and you know how to successfully market products to drive growth for your business.

The why isn't in question.

The only issue remaining is how to make it work as part of your day-to-day business operations from an actual implementation and technical perspective. Improving efficiency and output for our customers is what makes us so excited to showcase our seamless solution for selling on Amazon directly from BigCommerce.

With multi-channel retailing, one of the most common issues has always been the logistics — keeping track of orders and inventory across multiple touchpoints without bouncing between Excel and different software programs — all while trying to optimize each channel.

Maintaining this kind of incompatible system is a major drain on your finite time and bandwidth.

Beyond the inefficiencies, there are serious consequences when this patchwork solution inevitably fails or introduces unnecessary errors. BigCommerce has built a solution so you can simultaneously scale your Amazon sales and ecommerce shop from one central hub.

Our seamless integration with Amazon allows you to list products directly from your BigCommerce Control Panel without the aforementioned copying, pasting and merging of Excel spreadsheets and data exports across your entire company. Plus, with our two-way inventory sync, you'll always have an accurate snapshot of your entire inventory database — which updates in real-time.

Note: With Channel Manager, you can manage product listings for your online store, Amazon, Facebook, Google Shopping and Pinterest.

Selling on Amazon with BigCommerce

Read on to see how BigCommerce stores can be easily configured for selling on Amazon today.

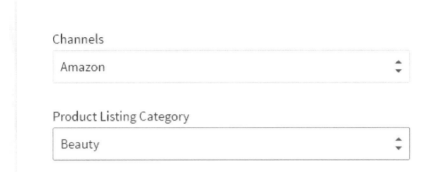

Requirements

Our requirements are broken out in 3 different subsections: Merchant Settings, Store Settings and Product Settings. For further details and examples of our integration in action, please go to the "How to Sell on Amazon with BigCommerce" section.

To use our Amazon Integration within Channel Manager, you must:

- **Have an Amazon Seller account on a Professional Selling plan**. If you don't have one, sign up at Amazon Seller Central.
- **Have a unique identifier (MPN or other standard ID)** for products not already available in Amazon's catalog.
- **Have at least one image per product.** The primary image of your product is called the "MAIN" image.
- **Enable Track Inventory** by Product and have a stock level greater than zero in order to initially list. Amazon listings that run out of stock will show as "Out of Stock" on Amazon.

For a full list of requirements, visit our Knowledge Base article about Selling on Amazon.

How to Sell on Amazon with BigCommerce

THE NEW PRODUCT LIST

Pick and choose which products are listed on your storefront and which are listed on Amazon. You can also manage product listings for all your other channels, like Facebook, Pinterest and eBay here as well.

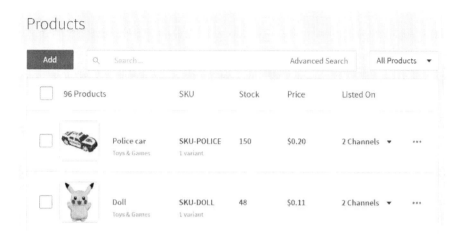

The new product list features a Listed On column that shows you which channels a product is included on, its current status (e.g. visible, pending, or rejected), and any errors that may be preventing the product from being included on a particular channel.

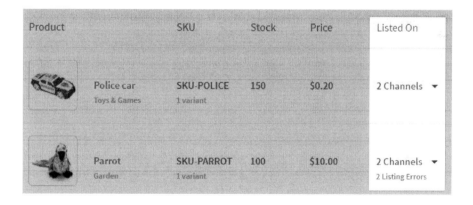

When you check one or more products, the Bulk Actions menu appears in the top right of the product list allowing you to edit, export, list, delete, or hide products en masse.

- Bulk edit selected
- Export selected
- List products on channels
- Hide products on channels
- Delete selected

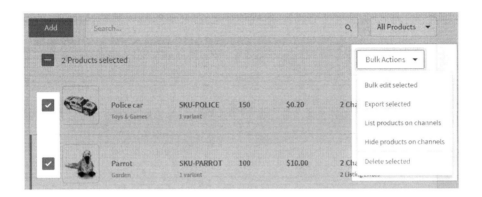

Managing Listings

CREATING LISTINGS

1. **Go to Products › View and click Storefront › Create Listing** next to the product you want to list on Amazon.
2. **Channels will set to Amazon**. Select a Product Listing Category.
3. **By default, your new Amazon product listing will use the same name,** description, brand and price details your product has in your BigCommerce store.
   a. Optionally, you can override these to be specific to Amazon. These edits are only reflected on Amazon.com – not on your BigCommerce store or other marketplace listings.
4. **Save your changes.** Once saved, your product will show an Amazon status of Pending. After your product has been successfully listed, its listing status will change from Pending to Active.

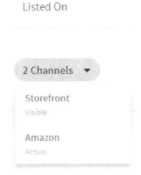

The Definitive Guide To Selling On Amazon

New and updated listings can take up to 30 minutes to appear on Amazon. Images can take up to 24 hours to appear on Amazon.

HIDING LISTINGS

To hide a product from Amazon, check the box next to it and select Hide products on channels from the Bulk Actions drop-down. Check the box next to Amazon, then click Hide products.

Checking Orders from Amazon

Orders received from Amazon are listed on your Orders screen with an Amazon icon.

Since billing is handled by Amazon, orders from Amazon come into your BigCommerce control panel with the shipping address also listed as the billing address when looking at the expanded order details.

Amazon does not include the real email address of the customer. Instead, they share an automatically generated anonymous email address. Per Amazon's policy, this address may not be used for marketing purposes.

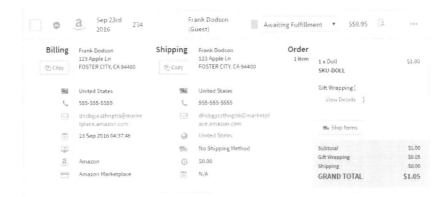

Partial shipments for orders from Amazon are not supported, so you won't be able to modify the quantity shipped when creating shipments for Amazon orders. Full and partial refunds are managed from your Amazon Seller Central dashboard.

Customer Experience on Amazon

Once your products are listed on Amazon, the browsing and checkout flows are controlled by Amazon. If your offering is featured in the Buy Box, your business is listed as the shipper and seller.

> Price: **$5.00** & FREE Shipping
> Note: Not eligible for Amazon Prime.
>
> In Stock. Ships from and sold by Glam My Mani.

If your offering is not featured in the Buy Box, you may be listed as an "Other Seller".

When a customer purchases one of your products, they will receive an email confirmation from Amazon. All order emails are handled by Amazon. Your new Amazon order is brought into your BigCommerce control panel, and they're shipped the same as you would any other order that comes in through your storefront. BigCommerce will update the order's status on Amazon when you create a shipment or change the order status.

Visit our Knowledge Base article about Selling on Amazon for Frequently Asked Questions and a complete breakdown of how to manage your Amazon listing.

Acknowledgments

This book would have been impossible to put together if not for all the hard work of so many people in the BigCommerce family around the world. You've seen the input and dedication of the authors in each chapter, but there were plenty of other people working behind the scenes.

Here's a big THANK YOU to every single one of them. From our executives to engineers to designers to marketers and everybody in between.

Brent Bellm, Cheri Winterberg, Casey Armstrong, Robert Alvarez, Alexandra Shapiro, Leo Castro, Ylan Kunstler, Paul Vaillancourt, Jimmy Duval, Russell Klein, Nate Stewart, Kevin Jones, Jennifer Reeves, Silas Godfrey, Aaron Bernard, Nina Blanson, Daniel Almaguer, Jon Wiese, Phillip Balli, Greg Stewart, Chris Marcocci, Angel Rodriguez, Arun Muralitharan, Ruth Adrinade, Zack Angelo, Jason Schmitt, Anthony Guriano, Stephen Meserve, Shannon Johnson, JOsh Burne, Pahul Pruthi, Alex Taylor, Brent Ric, Ziad Abdo, David Payne, Nataliya Solyani, Helen Feng, Cole Bennett, John Yarbrough, Leah Spector, Rachael Genson, Megan O'Brien, Andrei Kondratiev, Ian Carpenter, Sandeep Ganapatiraju, Nathan Booker, Chris Boulton, Bobby Martinez, Anthony Leach, Mark Ryan Shivers, Andrea Wagner, Brett Swihart, Ali Rastiello, Tiffany Tasa and Zach Rogers.

Printed in Great Britain
by Amazon